Tales of the Peak

by
Freda Bowman

Millstones.

P.P. 2006

NORTHEND 2006

Designed by Bob Brill and Freda Bowman
Front cover: Photograph of Magpie Mine by Bob Brill

ISBN No. 0-901100-66-8

With thanks to:

Roger Penney for his landscape drawings

Anne Bannister for her portraits

Kevin Gilfedder for his sketch of Stanage Edge

31/1/99 Stanage looking
South A above Pla

Contents

Foreword

Later this year, Bob and I plan to publish the third in our series of walking guide books - 'Brill Walks in the Peak'. These guides have taken almost all our spare time during the last two and a half years, but it has been time most enjoyably spent! Even more importantly, the results have been well received - our walks are being walked and are getting the thumbs-up!

An unusual feature of the guide books is the inclusion of a number of short tales, all based closely on the history of the areas covered. These are intended to make the walks themselves even more enjoyable, and it has been wonderful to hear that many people have found they do just that. As a result, we decided to bring the tales together into this single volume, which includes all those from 'Brill Walks in the Peak' books one and two, with the addition of two new, and slightly longer, tales.

Each one is spoken through the voice of a particular character - sometimes a real person from history, sometimes fictional. In all cases, the background has been very carefully researched, and an additional 'historical note' - giving a little more detail - follows each tale. I am grateful to Matlock Local Studies Library, for making this research a really pleasant task.

I do hope you enjoy reading 'Tales of the Peak'. Perhaps they may even encourage you to take a few walks in the beautiful Derbyshire countryside!

Very many thanks to Anne Bannister, for her stunning portraits, and to Roger Penney, for his beautiful landscapes. This would be a far lesser book without their efforts. Thanks must also go to Prof. Brian Robinson, for his advice, encouragement, and kind permission to use his photographs.

The Spa Lady's Tale

It was certainly not my decision that we should go there - it was
Humphrey's. It seems he had the right to make such decisions, in his role
of man of the house and sole provider. I had never before visited any part
of Derbyshire, had barely heard of Matlock. As for staying in a building
owned and run by a John Smedley, I had my fears. The name suggested
tradesman or mill worker (in this, of course, I was not wholly mistaken).
But as Humphrey put forward his reasons for the visit, I was considerate
enough to conceal the strength of my doubts. For some years, Humphrey
had suffered badly from rheumatism, and occasionally from gout. "Too
much rich food," our doctor had muttered, "and too little exercise." Not to
mention, of course, a family disposition. His parents - God rest them - had
scarcely been able to rise out of their chairs by the age of sixty.

Someone at the bank must have passed on to Humphrey that odd manual
which he brought home. 'Practical Hydropathy' by 'John Smedley of Lea
Mills', the heavy tome announced, 'including Plans of Baths' and 'Remarks
on Diet and Habits of Life'. Well, my habits of life were certainly not up
for scrutiny by any John Smedley, mill owner of Derbyshire. But
Humphrey's apparently were, not that he had ever heeded a word of
advice from me or from our doctor.

He proceeded to devour this ill-written manual and to discuss its contents
with the obsessive zeal of a religious convert. Hydropathy, Humphrey now
believed, was the answer to all his bodily ailments. This, of course, meant
weird water treatments of various kinds. Water was the cure, the salvation,
it would work the miracles that medicine could not. I myself felt the notion
to be completely absurd - I am not a doctor's daughter for nothing, and I
am not prone to be taken in by myth, magic or unscientific nonsense. Nor
was Humphrey, I had previously supposed. He was hardly a man of
romantic leanings, of that I had ample evidence. Indeed, he had always
shown a tedious degree of a reasoned judgement. But in this matter he was
won over, as so many others were, showing a pathetic trust in the curative
power of water.

Riber Castle

R.P. 2006

A decision was made before he had even reached the book's halfway point. We were to reserve a room at the great Smedley's Hydro in Matlock, Derbyshire. We would remain there for three weeks and he, at least, would submit himself willingly to whatever water treatments Mr Smedley considered appropriate. We would enjoy the simplicity and plainness of the food set before us, listen carefully to all advice given, attend a daily religious service and be in bed each night by ten o'clock at the latest. For these privileges, we would happily pay Mr Smedley two guineas each per week.

Just a month or so later, therefore, in early June of 1864, I accompanied him north, and not with good grace. For myself, I should have much preferred to go to the city of Bath, where at least good shopping and social entertainment would be on offer, along with the nonsense of the waters. Matlock, I suspected, would offer little of either. But Humphrey was fixed upon a retreat to this simple, northern village - I doubted it could be given a label of 'town'.

My mood was not lifted on our eventual arrival at Matlock Bridge Station, in a heavy downpour of rain. Fortunately the train journey had passed without problems. "If the worst comes to the worst," the thought struck me, "I can at least get myself back to London with reasonable ease." (A fake letter, concerning the illness of a relative, could be arranged if necessary.) A small carriage met us - a carriage from Smedley's met every train apparently. The elderly driver briefly introduced himself as Fred, and after heaving our considerable luggage aboard, proceeded to drive us up a frighteningly steep hill. I felt sorry for the two horses pulling our weight, their metal shoes sliding at times on the wet and uneven surface.

As we rose, 'Smedley's' loomed before us. A vast and dark stone building, far more imposing than I had imagined, but severe and brooding in appearance. If not an eyesore, then certainly not a thing of beauty. Despite my foreboding, I was aware of a certain curiosity. Whatever went on it in that place, it was performed on a grand scale. As we drew up to the entrance, at the rear of the building, Humphrey put some question to our driver, but the reply was unclear - heavily disguised in a strong Derbyshire brogue. In London, such speech would have aroused a curious amusement.

We were politely received in the huge entrance hall, and as Humphrey signed the arrival book, I noted the building's impressive, though plain, interior. Our bedroom turned out to be very spacious also, grand even, though completely without frills or special comforts. I have to admit that the view from its high windows, as the rain now cleared and the sky began to brighten, was impressive. Not that I am overly enamoured of views - they hardly provide merry entertainment. Before leaving us to ourselves (what a dreary thought that was), the steward, who had shown us to our room, felt obliged to issue a reminder concerning the House Rules. "No alcohol is allowed in any part of the building," he unsmilingly announced, without so much as a hint of apology. We were aware of this already, of course. Humphrey had accepted it as a necessary part of his cure. For myself, I had concealed a bottle of brandy inside my luggage and felt sure that a large tot would be needed that very night. "No sweet items should be consumed between meals," the fellow droned on. "Our meals are very wholesome and are always followed by stewed fruit or a simple pudding." Well, even Matlock boasted a few shops, I had noted. Humphrey could forego whatever he wished.

I have to say that first evening meal came as something of a relief. The food was indeed plentiful enough, though very plain - Mr Smedley, I was told, did not approve of either sauces or rich flavours. There were far more guests present in the huge dining room than I had foreseen - around a hundred, and it quickly became clear that people of good background from all over the country were present, and indeed from beyond. Tables were arranged in long rows and I found myself seated next to a very pleasing looking German gentleman, whose English was almost impeccable. Humphrey was seated at the other side of the table, but not quite opposite, so I felt perfectly justified in leaving him to his own conversational devices, which sadly were few.

Herr Schmidt, it transpired, was travelling on business throughout the north of England, and had decided that a week or so in the famous Matlock Hydro would be a pleasant interlude in an otherwise busy schedule. It soon transpired that he was staying there alone, though his domestic situation was not entirely clear. I immediately suspected he was a gentleman with an eye for the ladies. Nothing wrong with that, of course, provided it is accompanied by some charm, as indeed it was. Humphrey, for many years, had shown neither the eye nor the charm.

I was much amused to learn that Herr Schmidt had already fallen foul of the Smedley House Rules, by entering a lady's bedroom to return a silk scarf left on the sun seats outside. The lady in question, a widow, had been most appreciative, but this heinous deed had been spotted and reported by some beady-eyed steward. My German companion had been asked to pay a fine of half a guinea and been formally reprimanded. We were both highly amused by this, and I silently resolved that should I ever wish to see him in private, I would take greater care than had the luckless widow.

The dining occasion having been surprisingly pleasant, I felt a keen sense of disappointment when a tinkling hand bell drew the tables to silence. Then Mr John Smedley himself was announced, and an exceedingly ordinary looking man, probably in his sixties, rose from the other table and walked to the front, an open bible in his hand. He proceeded to read a - mercifully quite short - piece of scripture. This was not the end of it, however. No sooner had the bible closed and I had turned once again towards the fascinating Herr Schmidt, than Mr Smedley addressed us further. "I now wish to say a few words to the gentlemen present," he stated, "concerning the abominable practice of smoking." I hoped Humphrey would listen - his clothes always reeked of tobacco smoke and snuff.

Mr Smedley spoke with fervour and absolutely without trace of humour. As he returned to his place, I noted the woman I presumed to be his wife. Considerably younger than him, was my impression. A pleasant enough face, but no beauty. She had an air of piety around her - not at all the sort of woman, I imagined, that Herr Schmidt would be pleased to find himself seated next to. No doubt she and Mr Smedley were admirably suited. Probably very rich also, I now suspected, despite their gospel of plainness and simplicity.

Following this, many people wandered into the large and fairly comfortable sitting room. Card playing was strictly forbidden. We were expected to rest, not even to talk, perhaps to listen to some hymns from the piano. Again Herr Schmidt was a surprise. "Would you care to hear a little music?" he asked me, the slight accent quite disarming. "If you like, I will play for you." I did indeed like, and positioned myself smilingly at the end of a rather hard sofa, close to the piano. Humphrey, somewhat conveniently, had approached Mr and Mrs Smedley after the meal, and was engaged in earnest discourse with them. This was briefly interrupted a few minutes later, midway through the delightful playing of a Chopin waltz.

"Herr Schmidt," Mrs Smedley almost whispered to my friend, "we normally permit only sacred music to be played." "Madam," was his instant reply, "to me all music is sacred."

She withdrew with a slight blush. All my favourable impressions of the pianist were confirmed.

Whatever the nature of Humphrey's discussion with the Smedleys, it inspired him with even greater zeal for his forthcoming treatments. These would begin promptly at six thirty in the morning, when he would take himself along the corridor to bathroom number seven. His appointed bath man would then administer an extremely cold - just short of freezing - dousing of water all over the body, while Humphrey sat in a shallow tub of equally cold water. This would be followed by his being wrapped from head to toe in wet sheets, soaked in slightly warmer water. The whole process would take well over an hour, a time that I fully intended to spend asleep. Later in the day, two further treatments would be undertaken, probably involving the leg bath. Hot mustard poultices would be applied to his knee and ankle joints, these being his most severe problem areas.

During the middle part of the day, Humphrey informed me, he would spend time in the library or take a few gentle strolls with me around the grounds. Unless, of course, I decided to take a carriage with other guests into Matlock Bath and the surrounding countryside. This was unhesitatingly my preference.

Of course, there was a minor battle to be fought. The devout Mrs Smedley, it seemed, had charge of all women's treatments, and apparently she was expecting to have a consultation with me, to discuss any physical problems I might have. "Especially women's problems," poor, embarrassed Humphrey informed me. He was plainly anxious that I should avail myself of the kind offer. Naturally, I had no intention of doing so. The only woman's problem from which I suffered was a lack of entertaining male company, and this lack seemed likely to be unexpectedly relieved during our stay here.

Like Humphrey, Herr Schmidt availed himself of the water treatments - though only in the early morning, and involving nothing so drastic as mustard. He found the experience bracing, so he told me, though he shared my view that it was unlikely to cure any real ill. Indeed, he had no ills! He seemed to me to be in excellent health, possibly rather younger than myself, though I never inquired. It would have been irksome to have to lie. He regretted, he told me, that treatments were administered only by bath attendants of the same sex. On the Continent, it was inferred, things could be very different. It was not a suggestion he thought worthwhile putting to Mr and Mrs Smedley.

A coach and horses took us out most afternoons, though sadly always in the company of others. Most people spoke of Mr Smedley with great respect. A deeply religious man, I was informed, who himself had been won over to hydropathy after using it to recover from a serious breakdown. This breakdown, both mental and physical, had occurred some years ago, while the Smedleys were actually abroad on their honeymoon! ("What failures or disappointments had perhaps befallen them?" Herr Schmidt quietly mused). From the time of his cure, John Smedley had committed his life to hydropathy, and his devoted wife, Caroline, along with him. Early experiments were conducted on the workers in his textile mill and the vast Smedley building was the result of their apparent success. Many more centres had been set up by others, with his encouragement. Matlock Bank, as that hillside is known, was a veritable land of hydros, of which his own was the largest.

The departure of Herr Schmidt, a few days before our own (he had already extended his stay by more than a week), was deeply depressing, almost as much as Henry's enthusiasm with his new sense of wellbeing. I did have to admit that he looked better, though I felt convinced that forgoing drink, tobacco and large quantities of meat provided a much likelier explanation than wet sheets. Sadly, there is no simple cure for the personality.

My spirit of curiosity was lifted slightly by a surprise invitation to dine at the home of Mr and Mrs Smedley. Humphrey must indeed have impressed as a model patient. Home, as I already knew, was that Gothic pile, perched high above Matlock. None other than Riber Castle, on Riber Hill, designed and built by John Smedley for himself and his wife, just a couple of years previously. The rumoured cost was sixty thousand pounds.

So it was that we were conveyed that evening, by the Smedleys' personal carriage, up the cruelly steep lanes leading finally to their castle's entrance. The main door was positioned at the back of the building, to avoid bitter winds entering the house from across the Derwent Valley. The place was cavernous, chilly even on that pleasant evening of late June, though comfortably furnished and lit up, as the evening drew on, by gas lamps. These, we were told, were powered from a small gasworks, built nearby by Mr Smedley, for that very purpose. I wondered what possessed the two of them to choose to live in such a place, bereft even of the noise and company of children. Lack of children, of course, was something we all shared.

The table was generous, and the evening passed affably enough. I was again struck by the strength of John Smedley's convictions and by his desire to sway others towards them. This was not a man to allow a moment of self-doubt to alter his course, and his sense of being right was matched only by his utter contempt of the medical profession. His wife noddingly agreed with every word he uttered. His purpose was clearly her purpose also, and both seemed to work quite tirelessly. I have to admit I found them unappealing - intense and humourless - though part of me envied Caroline her strong drive and purpose. Women of wealth, at that time, had little sense of purpose in their lives, and much boredom. I myself was an example.

Of course, this was all a very long time ago, more than thirty years in fact. Mr Smedley died some twenty years ago, at the age of seventy-one, and I cannot imagine so unique a character in charge of a business now. Caroline died only two years ago. Surprisingly, we remained in touch during the eighteen years of her widowhood, a state I too was to enjoy for much of that time. During those eighteen years, she remained alone - unbelievably - in the vast and eerie Riber Castle, continuing her work as ardently as before. She was an admirable woman, but I have to admit to a great relief that she never accepted my occasional invitations to travel with me to the continent.

The great Hydro continues, now under different management, and far more relaxed, more luxurious. A far cry from the strict and spartan regime to which we submitted. In the future, it will no doubt be put to some other use. I cannot imagine that the silly myth of hydropathy will survive forever. I'm quite convinced it cured no one, and brought a much quicker end to more than a few!

As for Riber Castle, heaven knows what its future will be. Since Caroline's death, it has become a small boarding school for boys, but I cannot see that lasting long. Who would choose to send their son to such a desolate place? Though that's hardly a concern for me.

Should you ever find yourself in Matlock, you will hardly fail to notice its castle, looming over the place like a ghostly sentinel. It dominates that town as surely as its creator, Mr John Smedley, once did.

Historical Note

It has been said that John Smedley was the man who made Matlock. He certainly turned round the town's history when he built his great Hydro in 1853.

Smedley left school at fourteen, and for the next fifteen years he worked very hard to save his father's cotton mill from ever-threatening bankruptcy. Soon after marrying Caroline Harward, daughter of a Wirksworth vicar, he was struck down with a mysterious fever, which left him depressed and exhausted. After taking 'water treatment' at a clinic in Yorkshire, Smedley was overjoyed at his 'cure'. From that moment, he was a man with a mission! Plans to retire, on the profits of the now successful mill, were put aside. His workers were expected to act as guinea pigs - whether ill or not - and soon he began the huge (and in the opinion of many, very ugly) building on Matlock Bank.

His Hydro was tremendously successful and was soon taking in more than two thousand patients a year. Treatments included soaking, spraying, douches, wet sheets and mustard baths. Most were uncomfortable, and some probably dangerous to anyone in frail health. Local graveyards have been cited as good evidence of this! But at that time, most people believed fervently in 'water healing', and the rich were more than ready both to spend their money on such treatments and to endure the strict regime at 'Smedley's'. The lady who tells this tale is very sceptical, but she is not typical of her time. Her foreign friend's 'put-down' to Mrs Smedley, regarding sacred music, was actually made.

The great Hydro continued after John Smedley's death in 1874, along with others in Matlock. However, the whole idea became much less popular after the First World War and gradually most were converted into guest houses, schools and college buildings. Smedley's itself finally became the offices of Derbyshire County Council. Others have recently started new lives as very expensive, luxury apartments!

The Rutland Arms, pictured here, was built on the site of the White Horse Inn.

The Mill Owner's Tale

Father's funeral took place yesterday. Great pomp and ceremony there was, upwards of two thousand people lining the streets. All those heads bowed in silence as the black carriage passed by, some people even weeping. "You must feel so proud," an elderly man says to me, "a great man, that was, a very great man - brought well-being to thousands. And of course you, sir," he adds diplomatically, "are clearly following in his footsteps."

I'm unsure about that. I prefer to think of myself as my own man, but the sons of famous fathers can rarely attain that state. All the more difficult in my case, bearing his name - Richard - and following in the same business. It saddens me to say I was never close to him, although I am his only son and have but one half-sister. He was too enthralled by his work to be close to any human being, and that almost certainly included my mother. Did she die of purely physical causes, just a few months after my birth, thirty-seven years ago? Or was there just so little love, so little encouragement to stay alive? Many women die in childbirth, or soon after, you may well remind me. Perhaps my suspicions do him an injustice. It may be that she was taken by a fever, that she had not the strength to recover from a difficult birth. Perhaps the blow to him was so great, it put a coldness in his heart towards me. We never spoke of it. As a part of my early childhood, I remember him hardly at all. Later, he spoke to me only of cotton, of the mills, the machines, the workers. Of these I learned a great deal from my youth, and of course thanks to him I have long enjoyed wealth and lived in comfort. But never have I played the role of spoilt, incompetent son. In all honesty, I have a true mind for business and a sound enough judgement. Even he, who loved to have all things within his control, recognised that. He had no qualms about leaving me almost everything. I have long proved my worth to him and indeed I do not now intend to squander his work or his fortune. Riches offer a far better life than poverty, and I desire that my children enjoy good lives also.

Unlike my father, I have a large family. I feel such affection for every one of them that it is a puzzle to me that he could show so little affection for me. But as I have already indicated, he was not a man of feeling, and nothing counted for him as greatly as his work. My poor stepmother must have discovered this to her cost, and despite bearing him three daughters - of whom only my sister, Susannah, survives - she left him, and has now for some years lived with Susanna and her family. For the last few years of his life, my father was alone. I have to admit that I have seen him rarely during these recent times. The days were gone when I felt the need to consult him on business matters, and his views, which he always expressed in a greatly overbearing way, were not always my own.

I have not shed tears for him, but I shall ensure that the family honours his memory, and that what he gave to Cromford, to Bakewell, indeed to England, is not lost. He came from nothing, or at least from precious little. Youngest of a big family, no schooling, barely able to read and write - yet he gave to England a way of industry that is now making us great throughout the world. Never before in history has cotton, or anything else, been produced in such vast quantities under one roof. Of course, there are those who mourn the old ways, the cottage ways, but they will not return. My father has led the country to a different future.

Yes, of course it's all been so much easier for me, though he was a severe task master and had I not shown ability and usefulness he would, be assured, have quickly dispensed with my services. He was not a man to feel loyalty, if it went against the interests of his business. Friends, who had helped him in the past - lent him money, joined him as partners in various enterprises - were dropped promptly if he felt it advantageous to do so. 'Friends' is perhaps the wrong word, for a man like my father had use only for allies. Friends would always become an inconvenience. Several have, in the end, felt venomous towards him and probably with good cause.

I suppose, now, that Mary and I will leave Bakewell and move to Rock House in Cromford. The Cromford Works are larger than Lumford Mill, and I feel it right to be near them, though I confess I will miss this town greatly. Father set me up here fourteen years ago, and my mill has done wonders for the place. It was nothing but a poor and shabby village until then, held together by a few impoverished hill farmers and lead miners. It boasted nothing but a decent boys' school, set up by Lady Manners over a century ago. Nowadays the place can hold its head up.

I know that Mary has no wish to live in Rock House - father's old home, with its large window overlooking the mill, so that he could watch all the goings-on. Once Willersley Castle is finished, we will no doubt move in there - a huge mansion of a place, started by Father in his desire to show something for his wealth, but not finished in time for him. Of course, I understand my wife's reluctance. She knew father never approved of her, and indeed his words to both of us were scathing when our first child, Elizabeth, was born just four weeks after our wedding. No doubt he suspected Mary of seducing me, in order to secure a life of wealth, but if that were indeed the case, then what of it? I am content enough. He treated her, thereafter, with some scorn - an attitude that did nothing to improve my own relationship with him. And he has always seemed to take as little interest in his grandchildren as he once did in me.

Mary and I have eight children, six boys and two girls. She is happy, though I shall be pleased enough to see more. The Arkwright name is safe with me! Large families seem to me to be an altogether good and natural thing. Generally they are unavoidable in any case! Who would choose to lead a life of abstinence? Certainly I would not, but fortunately Mary is not the type of woman to suggest it. So I am confident there will be more. Of course, there is great risk in childbirth, especially if a woman is delicate in health. Thank God, Mary is strong and has always recovered quickly.

The mill women, too, seem sturdy and robust on the whole, and of course it is to a working family's advantage to produce many offspring, because each child can bring in good money. A family with six or more working children is obviously going to be far better off than one with two! Father always favoured employing whole families, but neither of us has ever taken orphaned or destitute children from the workhouses, even though they can provide almost free labour. Other mill owners have fewer scruples, especially up in Lancashire, when new mills seem to be opening up almost by the week. If a hundred children can be shipped up from a London workhouse, and then worked till they drop for nothing but a meagre bit of food and a couple of blankets, then it's a very fine profit to the owner, isn't it? It's even worthwhile for him to agree to take on a couple of imbecile children, along with every twenty sound ones.

I would never do such a thing. Father, to give him his due, rarely set a child on to work below the age of eight and insisted they had a bit of schooling first. His rule has always been that a child must be able to read a bit before starting work, though in honesty that rule is broken often enough. And usually it's broken because the child's parents will plead with us to take it on, able to read or not. Most parents can see no benefit to reading - not for children facing a working life in the mills.

Obviously my own children are in a quite different position. I intend to send all the boys to Eton, and thereafter to Cambridge. I desire that they feel completely at ease among people of wealth and rank. Father never felt such ease. Even when he was made Sheriff of Derbyshire five years ago, in 1787, and a little later became 'Sir' Richard, he expressed contempt for the aristocracy and never wished to associate with them. A poor childhood in Preston, without schooling, followed by apprenticeship as a barber, ill prepared him for an exchange of social graces! He was horrified to learn recently that I have lent the Duchess of Devonshire a significant sum of money, to cover her gambling debts. But I am well aware of the benefits of good connections.

But as for the large, hard-working families who serve us at Bakewell, and of course at Cromford, they have much to be grateful for. Men are employed as machine makers and repairers, and of course as overseers. Women and children work at the carding and spinning machines in our water-powered cotton mills. Father's famous water frame, perhaps the greatest technical advance of our time, is simple enough to be handled by a reasonably attentive child. I have always believed that he invented it, though others have claimed he stole the design, along with several more. Whatever the truth, no one ever made it work as he did, on such a scale, to such great profit. Even his enemies would have to admit he was the greatest industrialist in the world. Cromford has attracted families from miles around and many of them live in the good, sound houses that he had built for them. There's now a regular market, a church and a good-sized hostelry - the Black Greyhound. Working children are sent to Sunday School, boys one Sunday and girls the next. Is that not better than old lead mining families scratching a paltry living, in what was a desolate spot, offering nothing?

And here in Bakewell, as in other towns, it's much the same. Lumford Mill has provided plenty of work and this tiny place has grown beyond imagination since it was set up. Mary and I are treated with much respect in the town. I've got around three hundred and fifty workers, mostly women and children - there's less need for men, except as overseers, as we do little machine making here. But I've still built over fifty dwellings, and charge them out at a low rent. I'm particularly pleased with the cottages in New Square - the centre of the town now looks respectable and solid, and there's many a pleasant night to be had at the White Horse Inn. I know a good many of my workers by name. Not a bad lot, they are, though they need to be kept at their task. That's where the overseers come in. One woman has suggested to me that she, and other women, could fulfil such a role! That did amuse me. Women, by nature, will gossip and fritter away their time. Their fingers are nimble enough - better than a man's - but they can hardly be placed in a position of authority. The men would take it as an insult also.

Working shifts are certainly not overly long - twelve hours a day, six days a week - a lot better than some of the mills further north. There's a day and a night shift, of course - the machines are kept running continuously, though younger children generally only work the days. Two shifts are a boon to a lot of families. It means fewer beds are needed in their small houses and that gives people much more space to move around in.

Altogether, our workers have much reason to feel content and grateful, and judging by the turn out yesterday, most of them do. Up in Lancashire, there have been problems over the last few years - machines are getting smashed up by mobs, mills have even been set on fire. Father lost a brand new mill in Chorley that way. Do they really believe that without machines there would be work for all of them? As I said, the old days of cottage spinning will soon be gone for good. In any case, the population is now too great to be supported in that way. There are hordes of children everywhere you look, and their bellies are most likely to be filled through the efforts of people like my father and myself. Of course, father was very fearful for Cromford after that Chorley affair. He had a cannon set up to defend it, and plenty of arms and trained men at the ready, but we've had no trouble around here. People know there's far worse fates than working for Arkwright Mills!

If your wanderings take you round the town of Bakewell, spare a thought for my efforts, which helped to make the place handsome and prosperous. The town is now, of course, nothing more than a picturesque souvenir, a place for spending wealth, not creating it. The real world, the world of manufacture, moved away from here, as it did from Cromford, many years ago. It is the tourist, not the worker, who is important now.

Perhaps the lives of Arkwright workers would seem dreary and unrelenting to your mind. But there is certainly no ill in hard work, and their children did not starve. My own conscience is quite clear.

Historical Note

It is the son of Richard Arkwright who tells this tale - also called Richard, and only too aware that he stands in his father's great shadow of fame. Honesty compels him to admit the greatness of the older man's achievements, pivotal as they were to the Industrial Revolution of England.

Comparing the two of them as men, however, and especially as fathers, is a rather different matter. The younger Richard Arkwright, if less known to history, comes across in the records as a much more likeable character than the older one - a rounder, warmer personality, with a great deal more concern for those close to him. He appears to have been, first and foremost, a family man, revelling in his children's company, always remaining close to them and giving to them very generously (eleven children were born to him and Mary).

He was also, however, a shrewd businessman, amassing a great fortune in his own right. As an employer, Richard was reasonably enlightened for his own time, if not in our eyes. But unlike his father, who focussed on cotton production, Richard the younger diversified into many areas - banking, property, stocks and shares (including shares in Turnpike Roads) and money lending to the aristocracy. In part, this was because he faced much stiffer competition than his father. Lancashire was by then the heart of the cotton industry. Cromford had become isolated and rather out of date.

Cromford Mill finally closed in 1846. Now owned by the Arkwright Society, it is an interesting place to browse around. Bakewell's Lumford Mill was sold to the Duke of Devonshire in 1860 but burned down a few years later. Richard Arkwright the younger died in 1843, at the good age of eighty-seven. He had outlived his wife by sixteen years.

The Lead Miner's Tale

Ay sir, sit th'sen down - no problem at all. Pub's full just now, full all day it is, full every damn day! No one sits at a table on 'is own any more. Make th'sen at 'ome.

Oh Lord no, it's not always like this. Place were a lot quieter till a couple o' weeks back. Never empty, mind. There's always some men just off their shift, or else waitin' to start one. Take it tha's not from round 'ere? Just passin' through? Well, tha's found us at a bad time. Miserable faces everywhere tha looks, must 'ave noticed as much. Just as well we've a decent pub to be sat in - and there's another one down road that'll be just as full. Not many spendin' a lot on the beer, mind. Everyone's missus would be waitin' at 'ome with too much to say. All of us in same damn boat, though, that makes it a bit easier. A man can do a lot o' talkin' over a pint o' warm beer that's been sittin' in front of 'im for well over an hour. All miners, in 'ere, o' course, every damn last one of us. Not th'sen, though. Tha's not got the 'ands of a miner!

No doubt tha'll be wonderin' what I'm ramblin' on about. It's the Mill Close - that's where the lot of us work - or did. Not that we're likely to ever get down there again. It's 'ad it, 'as that place, final curtain. Probably just as well there's a war brewin', or so a lot o' folks is sayin'. It'll give a few o' these youngsters some'at to do, at least. Won't do owt for me, an' not for thee neither, I'd say. Did my stint in last one. Bloody 'ard stint it were an' all! Thought we'd put paid to all that nonsense over there.

Mill Close? Well, tha certainly wouldn't be askin' that, not if tha came from round 'ere, I can tell thee! It's a lead mine. Not that we 'aven't found plenty of other stuff down there over all them years, but lead's the real thing. Biggest producer in England, she is, in fact biggest in 'ole o' Europe. At least there's plenty stocked up to make every bullet they're ever likely to need, if this bloody war starts up. Just like we made most of the damn bullets for that last war! There's lead mines all over place round 'ere, and there used to be an 'ole lot more - scores of 'em!

"THE MINERS STANDARD"
WINSTER

R.P. 2006

Does tha know that a couple of 'undred years ago there was more than twenty mines just round Winster? But our Mill Close were the very best of 'em. That were when most o' this village were built, and it 'ad more than twenty inns an 'all! Not quite as good in that way now. But as I said, there's never been a mine what's a patch on Mill Close, nowhere near it! Gone through some bad times, she 'as, but these last few years there's been no lookin' back. Everywhere we turn there's a new vein looms up, and each one's better than one we worked before. There's tons and tons of that stuff still down there - God knows 'ow much - not that we'll ever be gettin' it out now. It's there to stay.

What's problem wi' it? 'Ole damn place is flooded, that's what. This man, by name o' Fred, well 'e drills through into a river, or maybe it's a lake, right down in depths o' mine. Not 'is fault, understand, could 'ave been any one of us. Well, wall weakens a bit and now there's 'undreds o' thousands o' gallons an hour coming in, so I'm told. Nowt pumps can do against that, not even our Jumbo - that's what we call biggest one. There's been plenty o' floodin' down there in my lifetime, but never owt like this! Can't see 'em ever getting' it workin' again, not this time. Miracle no one were killed. All got us sen out in time, a lot of us just by skin of us teeth. Thought I were going to join me grand-dad at one point. 'E was drowned down a mine. Not an unusual thing, that, specially in 'is day.

Oh ay, it's always been dangerous work, tha's right there. Men's work - tha'd not get a woman down a mine, not on thy life. Not that anyone'd want 'em! Only places you can get away, down there and in 'ere. It'd be one 'ell of a life if they got everywhere. There's a real good feeling 'mong us men, real pals, never let anyone down. Proper men, they are, not frightened of a bit o' dirt and sweat - proper 'ard men. Not bothered about danger neither, and there's always a good chance o' floodin', or else of a roof cavin' in, that's another one. Thing is with a roof, if it do cave in, then tha's not going to be frettin' about it for too long - short and sharp, that's what it'd be! 'Appened to a good pal o' mine, not that long back. Sad thing was, fella 'ad just 'anded 'is notice in an' all. Mind thee, there's not been so many accidents in recent times, not like it were in days past.

Tha what? Oh no, wouldn't want to work anywhere else, to be honest. Probably couldn't do owt else, not now. Not after all them years down there. Went straight back down after last war, and I'd already been down a good few years before it. War came at a good time, as a matter o' fact.

Would 'ave been laid off anyway - lead ore were running out just then - or so they all seemed to think. Weren't the case, as it turned out. Place 'as kept me in work ever since, though a good few years back, round 1929, they thought it were running out again. Then this big company - Consolidated Gold Fields of South Africa, it calls itself - puts in a real lot o' money. Bought us biggest electric pumps in the world. That meant we could go a lot deeper. So go deeper we did, and there it were! Richer ore than any we'd ever seen in all our born days. Gold Fields were a good name for it! Lot better than real gold, if th' asks me.

What's them pumps for? Well, they're pumpin' water out o' course, what else? Water's always been the big problem, it's the problem in all lead mines, but specially in that one. And the deeper we go, the worse it gets. We're usually workin' ankle deep in muddy water, knee deep, many a time. And o' course, even in drier bits, it's always slippery underfoot. That's what we all wear clogs for - might seem odd to some folk, but clogs is safest thing. What tha does is, tha takes a pair of old boots to a good cobbler's and 'e'll make 'em into clogs by putting on proper wooden soles, with nails and clippets. But o' course, all this water, them pumps 'ave to cope with it, get rid of it. They channels it off through long tunnels - soughs, we call 'em. If it weren't for them there's not a lead mine around what could be worked. If pumps can't cope wi' it - say in a thunderstorm - then tha's got to get th'sen up damn quick! But them big pumps can get rid o' thirty million gallons a week. That's 'ow we've managed to get down so low - 'undred and twenty-five fathoms, and deeper. And all that good stuff lies very deep. If tha wants it, tha's to get down for it!

Ay no, it's not lit up, not most of it. Bottoms o' shafts is lit, but all rest's dark - that's what we get candles for. Every man gets five candles a shift, and there's about an 'undred and thirty of us on each shift, and there's three shifts a day. That's one 'ell of a lot o' candles! On some levels there's gas about, so if tha needs to go there, tha gets a safety lamp. No one lights a ciggy up round them parts, neither! Course there's a no smokin' rule everywhere in mine, but it's not usually kept to. I've never kept to it m'sen. We can see a boss comin' from way off - can see light from 'is torch - no candles for that lot! Plenty o' time to stub out.

Tha's got to remember - it's maybe not something tha'll know, not bein' familiar wi' minin' - that a man's not likely to be workin' near a shaft, not near main shaft anyway. That's the one the men get lowered down in, in a cage. I've got nearly two mile to walk once I'm down, to get to where I'll be workin'. Down main shaft, along a level, then I've to climb on rungs down another shaft - no cage there to lower me - then walk along again, and so on. Takes a good bit o' time in shift, just to get out there, and then back again. I take snap down wi' me, and some-one'll be brewin' tea. No comin' back up for any meal break - it'd take much too long. Can't come up for lavatory neither! Don't do to be too fussy, down a mine! Once a vein's been found, no one ever knows 'ow far it'll be goin'. A vein goes sideways, like a long pipe, and we follows it as far as it goes, if we can. There's no way of knowin' when it's goin' to peter out.

No, work never stops down there. Goes on all round clock, every day o' week. Three shifts, there are - done 'em all in me time but I like night shift best - quarter to ten at night till quarter to six in mornin'. Wife gives me a decent breakfast, then I'll be in bed around quarter past seven, and I get bed to m'sen an' all. It suits me and it suits 'er, does that. Very long time since we've wanted owt different. Then I'll be asleep till 'bout two, bit longer if she don't set about wakin' me up by clatterin' around. Like to do a bit o' gardenin' in afternoons. It's only a patch, but it's alright for a few carrots and cabbages. Get dinner about five, if she 'asn't spent all afternoon gossipin'. Beats me what women find to natter about. It's about nowt, usually, but that never seems to stop 'em!

No, it's not too bad a life. That mine 'as looked after Winster well enough, and a few other villages besides. When tha thinks of all them folk what's been laid off in towns, or 'avin' to take wage cuts! Won war, didn't we and then what do a lot o' folk get for it? No money, no jobs, no nothin'. And now it looks as if the 'ole bloody mess is goin' to start again! The laugh is, some German company's just offered to drain this mine for us, so I've 'eard. Claim they've got better stuff to do it than we 'ave. But that Goldfields lot - and they've got all the say-so now - they've told 'em no thanks, and in no uncertain terms. Too many nasty things goin' on over there. They don't want owt to do with 'em. Whether our lot'll manage to drain place out is another thing. Doubt it very much, mesen. And that's nearly eight 'undred men out, what with smelter as well. 'Cos smelter's no damn good to anyone, not without mine.

Four 'undred years, that's 'ow long Mill Close 'as been goin'. It's the only reason why Winster exists! That mine's brought this place some real riches over the years - tha's only got to look at some of them fancy buildings in the 'igh street, and then all them cottages up on this 'ill. And now it all looks as if the 'ole damn lot's at an end.

Well cheers sir, I will an' all! Throat's gone dry, what with all this talkin' - 'ope I've not bored thee to death. It's not often we see a new face at Miners Standard. Ay, another pint'd go down a real treat!

Historical Note

Lead has been mined in the Peak District since Roman times, and throughout the centuries it has been the backbone of the area's economy. The Mill Close Mine, near Winster, was the most productive of all, though in fact its greatest era was not until the 1930s - a time when lead mining in this country was drawing to its close.

In 1938, men working in the Mill Close Mine accidentally drilled through into an underground lake or river, and it took many months to pump the flooded mine clear. It finally closed in 1940, with over two thousand litres a minute still pouring in.

Lead miners were always renowned for being heavy beer drinkers. The traditional belief was that beer helped to protect them from lead poisoning. The Odin Mine, which is the subject of this verse, was near Castleton, one of hundreds of lead mines once worked in the Peak District.

'Come fellows drink - drink, drink your fill,
Full soon we must gang up the hill
Where Odin, rich in shining ore
Shall give us glasses - hundreds more;
Then luck to Odin - golden mine,
With metal bright, like the sun doth shine.'

The Lover's Tale

Sometimes I stand a while beside his grave - an unusual monument altogether, though simple enough, not showy. Thomas Bateman, renowned archaeologist and antiquarian, beloved by his family and held in deep affection by his friends. A man who knew his vocation, who sensed what should be done with his life. And one day, the most important thing he needed to do was to be well rid of me.

A sudden event, that was. Perhaps I'd always had a fear of it, but never truly allowed myself to expect it. Desperately happy, we always were, in each other's company. Thomas passionate and intense in his hunger for me, and I certainly no less so in my need for him. But there was more than lust between us. He had willingly confronted both public condemnation and his grandfather's anger in order to be with me, laughing scornfully at such reactions, as often as not. We were young. We were free beings, Thomas and myself, or so both of us believed - unrestrained, casting aside a stuffy convention, indifferent to the narrow, stunted opinions of others.

But not indifferent to the stark terms of a will. A will carefully worded by his grandfather, the man after whom my Thomas had been named. The old man died in the May of 1847, at the good age of eighty-seven. My own Thomas was just twenty-five. The funeral respectfully conducted, I witnessed him listen attentively as the conditions of inheritance were read to him - and with his own father long dead, that inheritance concerned Thomas alone. A change appeared in the eyes of the man who loved me, a subtle, distant change but one which instantly sealed my fate.

The words were more direct, more personal, than you might expect a legal document to express. Thomas was to end his 'criminal connection' with me. If he did not, his benefit in the estate 'shall absolutely cease and be void'. And there was to be little time of grace, the will set an absolute deadline of three months. Thus, by the twenty-sixth of August 1847, I was to be removed entirely from his life. And the recompense? It was total ownership of the Middleton Estate. This, of course, included Middleton Hall, the Georgian mansion built by his grandfather. It encompassed Lomberdale

Hall - our own home - and land of around three thousand acres. Not least, it would bring to him the almost feudal service and respect of the villagers. People for whom we had long been a subject of malicious gossip.

You may already be hardening against Thomas in your heart. Perhaps unjustly. Who would not do the same? Would I, in that position, have not done the same? He could not marry me. The problem was not one of class, though in this matter I stood well below him. I was a married woman already - wife of Mr Mason, a boatman on Cromford Canal.

Perhaps I should take you back a little further, even into Thomas's life before the time I entered it. Thomas's mother, Mary (a name I share), died when he was a mere nine months old and she herself only twenty-two years. His father, William, was grief-stricken and moved with his baby son from their home in Rowsley, to live with his own father at Middleton Hall. More than ample room, of course, though a sad lack of female influence. Perhaps the three got on well enough together - Thomas always said they did. Indeed, the older Thomas is quoted as describing his little grandson as 'one of the finest children ever born'. William was lucky, despite the tragic loss of his wife. He shared a fine home, had no worries for money, he could choose his activities. Earlier in his youth he had developed an interest in antiquity, encouraged by the huge library at Middleton Hall. From this came the thrill of digging up several of the area's mysterious barrows - ancient burial grounds of our forgotten ancestors - forcing them to yield their secrets to the fork, the spade, the pick. My Thomas accompanied him from a very early age, the quiet father and the far more assertive son uniting in this love of earthy exploration.

But William was not strong. Years of failing health - I don't think Thomas ever truly knew the cause - brought on his death at the age of forty-eight. Now there remained only grandfather and grandson, two men of the name Thomas, aged seventy-five and thirteen, both of them very determined characters. The younger man retained his interest in the digging, in unearthing our primitive pagan past. On holiday from the boarding school in Liverpool to which he was sent, he roamed the woods and moors with a companion, William, while at the same time devouring, as his father did before him, the works in his grandfather's library. Thomas and William became inseparable, though Thomas had an intellect far beyond that of his friend. Digging up the fascinating pieces from beneath the burial mounds could never have been enough. They must be examined, measured, documented, understood. Theories must be proposed to explain them. This was a rich science, and it began to carry his name far beyond the boundaries of the place he lived.

But I must enter here. A few years later, Thomas's eyes chanced upon me, and our physical delight in each other took hold with suddenness and consumed us both in its thrall. I doubt at first he asked himself if I might be already married. It was some time before I told him, because in truth it barely seemed to matter. I was young, without a child, my husband an easily content man without insight or suspicion. He made little fuss when Thomas, after receiving a part of his father's money at his coming of age, obtained a small house for the two of us in Bakewell. As our life together became known, the only wrath expressed was that of the older Thomas, enraged and humiliated. But my Thomas remained defiant, confident of his grandfather's deep sentiment for him. They had already known many differences of opinion - fiercely expressed - but never had his financial means been cut off and nor were they now. Deaf to the pious voices around us, he lay entirely under my spell.

I am sure others believed it would end within a few months at most - just as long as it took for a young man's passion to be fully satisfied and to start its ebb. We defied them. Many months later, we moved from Matlock Street, Bakewell, to Thomas's newly-built house in Middleton, Lomberdale Hall. Here we were to live for three more years. For quite some time, my sister joined us there, a generosity that seemed to fire the local gossips even more.

In the September of 1844 - to my great delight - we travelled together to Canterbury for the first great Congress of the newly formed British Archaeological Association. Outside the narrow confines of Middleton, of course, we were presumed to be man and wife. The following year, we toured in leisurely style around the North, partly for Thomas to visit the huge excavations then taking place around York. Again, not an eyebrow was raised.

Why could it not continue? Of course it could not. Had there been a child, perhaps that might have saved me, but I was not fertile, a fact for which Thomas was no doubt grateful.

There was no time for him to lose. He had to tell me his decision, but of course I knew of it already. I shed not a tear in his presence, I am proud enough in nature, if not in birth. Within two days I chose to leave, though not penniless - he was an honourable man. Since that moment I have not set my eyes closely upon him, not once. But I have never lived far away, and I have known much of his doings. Especially in the weeks that followed.

Thomas decided to marry quickly. Marriage was not a condition of the will, but perhaps he sensed that respectability must be promptly restored. There existed no one else he loved - quite obviously not - but there was at Lomberdale a young housekeeper, twenty-two years old. Not a beautiful woman, and little higher in status than me. The sister of his barrow digging friend, William Parker. Sarah must have been shocked indeed to receive his offer, but I doubt she hesitated long. Advantages can be quickly weighed up. On August the second, the two were married at Bakewell register office, and a few days later he was formally handed the keys to Middleton Hall and its beautiful estate. On that occasion, the happy pair were driven in their carriage through the village, where there was feasting and celebration, free ale at the Bateman Arms, and a huge bonfire as the evening drew on. Thomas was now truly the country squire, a man of substance. The following year, unsurprisingly, Sarah gave birth to his first child.

I do not seek to sound bitter. Without such conformity, such observance of the rules, he may never have achieved what he later did. We did not live in a world of choice. A sense of freedom during youth was little more than acting out a fantasy. And he did achieve, did Mr Thomas Bateman, aided by an undemanding wife who supported him quietly and unquestioningly, who laid no claim to any ambition or wants of her own. His energies were freed and both the excavations and studies grew apace.

Thomas revealed the secrets of not scores, but hundreds of prehistoric burial grounds - on a scale no longer possible and with a freedom that would no doubt be the envy of any archaeologist of a later time. There were no rules, no restrictions, no hard won permission to be sought, no hand of authority involved. But Thomas was not a common grave robber. 'Barrow digger' was not a term of abuse used against him, though of course his methods and tools could only be those of the time. No doubt to your own age his ways would seem crude, even greedy. He was, however, meticulous. The skulls, the bones, the urns and the ornaments he found were carefully preserved in the rapidly growing collection at Lomberdale Hall. Each one he painstakingly examined, against the background of his vast reading and knowledge. They were minutely documented in his papers. And not only did he engage in the digging himself, along with his group of trusted companions, but Thomas organised many other excavations in Yorkshire and Staffordshire. Middleton came to be seen, so I read, as a pioneering centre within English archaeology. Our lovely Lomberdale Hall was almost doubled in size to house his work. Alongside, of course, the growing number of his children.

Thomas was fortunate. Wealth means freedom to pursue the activities you choose, profitable or not. In justice to him, he seemed a much liked man, even in his guise as arch Tory landowner (such very different views from his Liberal father). He had a little school built for village children, though other than this little changed in Middleton. Occasionally villagers have been invited to eat, drink and make merry at his expense. I am acquainted with people who attended such a party, as the Crimean War finally drew to its close. At least three hundred villagers took tea in the gardens and a very great quantity of ale was drunk.

I think it was in the autumn of 1850 that I heard Thomas was very ill, indeed that he was expected to die. He did not die, perhaps helped by the hasty arrival of an eminent specialist from London. I am not aware of what the illness was, but recovery from it seemed to make Thomas far more religious than before. I heard he was seeking to atone for the sins of his past, a suggestion that caused me no little pain, even after so very many years. Thereafter, he became a strict non-conformist, in the steps of his grandfather. A faithful pillar of that institution, in both prayer and financial generosity.

In August 1861, Thomas died. There had been a sudden illness - again I am ignorant as to its cause. I understand his life ended in a serious haemorrhage, very early on a dull and wet morning. He was thirty-nine, and had achieved much, but it is cruelly young for such an intellect to be destroyed.

I often wonder if he was happy. There must have been satisfaction in his work, and perhaps that was what truly mattered to him. Sarah gave birth to five children, but to only one son, named Thomas William. From the day

I left, I sense a great dullness settled itself over his life, an indifferent acceptance of social requirements. Perhaps I am mistaken, I am hardly unbiased.

Sarah died just a year ago, and only five years after Thomas. The good age reached by his grandfather was certainly not enjoyed by those who followed. She is buried here also, a fact which kept me away for a time, but now it seems of less matter. Young children were left without their parents - the youngest, Clara Theodora, was but three years old. I believe Sarah's younger sister lived at Lomberdale for some time, just as mine did. Perhaps she shoulders some of the care. Their son, Thomas William, must be about fifteen now. Like my Thomas, he finds himself alone at a sadly young age. I hear he is not a boy of his father's character and that he is querulous with his four sisters. It seems he has no interest whatever in the past, but indeed is showing little sense of any future path of his own. I feel a sympathy for the lad, even a desire to see him, to talk with him, though that is almost certain never to occur. I am sure my name has long been blotted out from every memory and certainly from all mention. I am the woman who never was.

If you are strolling through Middleton, take the overgrown path that leads along to Thomas's grave. You will hardly be impressed - it is plain and rather neglected. Perhaps someone will one day give of their time to make the place a little more welcoming. The grave lies on a pleasant hill, close to his home, and seems known to but few. Thomas set out in his life to reveal the secrets of the dead, the dead of a forgotten world, and this task he fulfilled. Few men are fortunate enough to know such fulfilment. Perhaps there should be no sadness for his life, not even inside my own heart.

Historical Note

I first came across a book about the life of Thomas Bateman in Matlock Local Studies Library - always a pleasant and welcoming place to do research! Quite rapidly, I found myself rather more fascinated by Bateman's personal life than by his considerable achievements as an archaeologist.

Bateman lived from 1821 to 1861, and pursued his brief, but very productive, career with almost obsessive vigour. Sometimes known as 'The Barrow Knight', he dug up more prehistoric burial grounds and unearthed more artefacts, in both Derbyshire and Staffordshire, than has ever been managed before or since. The vast majority of his finds he kept in his own mansion, Lomberdale Hall, near Middleton-by-Youlgrave. However, this huge collection was later to be sold off by Bateman's only son, who also squandered much of his father's general wealth. Fortunately, an important part of the collection, as well as many documents and letters, was bought by Sheffield Museum.

The rather sad 'Lover's Tale' is told through the voice of Mary Ann Mason, Bateman's lover, and the sharer of his home, for several years. He could not marry her, and indeed he rejected Mary ruthlessly when it became expedient to do so. Thereafter, her part in his life seems to have been completely unacknowledged. I understand that when Sheffield Museum received Bateman's letters and notes, the name of Mary Ann Mason had been cut or blotted out from every line in which it had once appeared.

It is pleasing to be able give Mary a new breath of life here!

A View from the Hut

I made it good and clear to George from the start. There was no chance at all that I'd be running any lodgers' hut! No doubt plenty of other women are prepared to cook breakfast for eight men - plus their own husband - well before six o'clock in the morning. So let them get on with it, they're more than welcome to the bit of extra money that comes their way. Nor was I going to be cleaning up a sour smelling bedroom, emptying fag trays and getting rid of empty bottles from under eight beds, as well as sorting through piles of smelly sheets and workmen's clothes. And the whole lot next to my own living room, which of course they'd all be sharing! That's to say nothing of the lot of them in and out all day long, depending on their shift, wanting cups of tea and plates of potatoes and God knows what. "Count me out of that," I says to George. "We'll manage well enough on your wages, and what we can't have, we'll do without. I'm no stranger to doing without."

Some of those men are rough in their ways, not surprising when you look at what their lives have been. It takes more than a week in the doss house - and that's where all single workmen have to stay when they first arrive - to sort them out. Well, they may be disinfected and checked for disease in there, but it's not a school for good manners. Mind you, it's amazing how a lot of them improve, once they're in a decent household and being looked after a bit. It's best if the woman's strong-minded and not prepared to take a single word of abuse or any loutish behaviour. That's a job I could tackle well enough, no doubt, if I was prepared to take it on.

So that was that. The hut we've lived in, since we landed up here around seven years ago, in 1903, is smaller than the lodging ones, but bigger than some of the others. The smallest ones only get the one bedroom - they're the huts for married couples without families. There's only a few of those been built, probably for the good reason that not many people can stay in them for too long. From the day of a wedding, you're lucky if it's more than the year before the first one arrives. Certainly wasn't any more in my case.

Our hut's an inner one in a block of four - top road, number 52. Not a bad spot to live, in fact a bit bigger than the one we had in Wales. There's a really good-sized living room - it's eighteen foot six by thirteen foot - then a

Wash day at Birchinlee - by kind permission Prof. Brian Robinson

pantry and a decent scullery with water laid on, piped in from Bank Clough. We've got a couple of bedrooms, one for us and Violet, and one for the lads. They'll all be having to share in a week or two, Violet's about old enough to be moved out from our room. If she still wakes up in the night - and she's been by far the worst one for that - then Bob should be able to talk her off again. He's a kindly lad, with a great deal more patience than I've got!

The rent's six shillings and sixpence a week, which isn't daylight robbery, and we get three hundredweight of coal every week for that as well. It's a Richard Hardwick that collects rents every week from each hut - the Village Superintendent, as he likes to be known. Pompous man, in my opinion. Very important, he seems to think he is, marching round, knocking on doors and looking for problems. He has to see that the toilets are working properly as well, though you can see him making a point of screwing his nose up when he goes inside. And it's not as if most of us don't work damn hard to keep them clean. Serves him right that as soon as his back's turned, everyone calls him 'shit house Dick'!

Violet's the first one we've had born here at Birchinlee. Just over a year ago - fifth of April 1909, to be exact. Delivered by old Granny Brown, like they all are here. Doctor only wants to get involved if your life's hanging by a thread. Not that I'd got away with it, in the few years we were here before she came along, not at all. Two of them I lost, on the trot. The first wasn't too bad, only three months along and it was all over without a lot of trouble, though it does leave you feeling very low. Second time was a lot worse - I was a good five months down the line. Very painful, that one was, took me long time to feel right afterwards, and I bled badly for weeks on end. Of course there was no rest, none at all. How can you rest with three young lads and a husband who labours hard all day and needs a decent meal when he comes in? George isn't the demanding sort, I've got to be fair to him, not like a lot of them. He even helped me get the lads washed and put to bed if he came off an early shift. There's not many around who'd be willing to do that. But there was no way he could take any real burden off my shoulders, and we had no family around to do it either. George comes from Lincolnshire - the Derwent Valley, in north Derbyshire, might as well be on another planet. My own family are Welsh, of course, through and through, so nothing doing there either, though there's not one of them I'd have been too pleased to see in any case. So we were on our own and I just had to get on with it. Plenty of neighbours, of course, just like in Wales, but I'd sooner not get over-involved with neighbours.

There's a very narrow line between being friendly and being plain nosy, and most people are nearer the nosy. George has got a lot more time for neighbours than I have. He quite enjoys a bit of banter and a laugh, and he doesn't seem to cross people as much as me. So I leave it to him to do the chatting, and put up with their endless moans. They like him for that, of course, especially the women. I've got no time at all for moaners.

It's hard to keep yourself to yourself here. We're in the depths of the country but the huts are tight packed along the two main roads of the village. Not a village as you'd imagine one, mind. Forget the cosy inn, the old church, the cottages, the little tea shop. This is a village for workers, thrown up specially for them, intended just for the time they're doing an important job and likely to be pulled down as soon as that job's done. There's about a thousand of us packed in here. And there's no frills, no one's tried to make anything look pretty. In fact it looks like an army camp from a distance, because the walls of every hut - and all the other buildings too - are covered with corrugated iron. That's where its usual name comes from - Tin Town - though the proper name's Birchinlee, after a farm it was built near. And there's nowhere in this place where you can't hear the banging and hammering from the works, all day long and a lot of the night. It's some distance away but we've no escape from it.

It's a different story inside the huts, of course. Richer folk would no doubt turn their noses up, but strangers often get quite a surprise if they happen to be invited to walk through a front door. The huts are all wood-lined and every one's got a big Derbyshire fireplace, with a full cooking range. Then there's a dresser and a good-sized table. A lot of people have saved up over the years to get themselves some nice plates and cups and the like, and they make sure they can be seen. I've a few bits on show myself. And there's always plenty of family photographs on the walls, usually with wooden frames. We might be navvy families - and that's a term of abuse in the mouths of many people - but we can live proper lives and behave in a decent way like anyone else. I'm very strict with my three lads. They know to do as they're told and they know not to answer back, and I don't need to threaten them with their Da's belt either. I'm quite prepared to take a belt to them myself, if it needs to be done. Probably a good bit harder than George would do it, as well.

Little Violet's already got a sparkle in her eye. I've a feeling she'll have her Da and her brothers round her little finger before too long. George's face lights up at the very sight of her, when he comes in. She'll not be getting too much of her own way with me, there's no fear of that, but I will admit to being pleased when she came along - a girl at last, to say nothing of seeing her a good size and healthy, after losing those other two. I look at her asleep sometimes, and I think 'I hope you get an easier life than me'. I'd like her to have better schooling than I did - that shouldn't be too hard. And I'd rather she married a good bit later than me as well. Find someone with a few pennies to rub together, not have to scrimp from one year's end to the next! Not that she's likely to listen, of course, not if she turns out as headstrong as her Mam. I was determined to be married young and get away from home, never thought twice, once I could see George was falling for me. I was about as tough as girls come, but I could recognise decency when I saw it. Don't know now, though, what all that blasted hurry was about. I've barely drawn my breath since.

It's another massive job the men are on here, another huge dam - in fact two dams, by the time they've done. I say 'another' because that's what a good few of them, including my George, were building in mid-Wales, and we had a set-up over in the Elan Valley not unlike this village here. The huts were very much the same, except they were wood-boarded, not covered with corrugated iron like these. And the place was even further out in the back of the beyond, if that's possible. So we're well used to the open hills, the raw winds, the spiteful winters, and we're also well used to living in a tin pot set-up in the middle of nowhere. This one might be called Tin Town, but you'd be disappointed if you came all the way up the valley expecting to see a town.

Some of the families have seen far worse conditions, mind, especially the single men, the lodgers. A lot of them have had working lives you'd never believe. They've had to sleep in whatever damp old shack they could find a space in, and even out in the open, often enough. Riddled with lice, they usually are, when they roll up at the doss house. That place has to be kept well disinfected, and the men need to be cleaned up and often get their heads shaved before they're allowed to take any lodging in the village. They've been used to working for bosses that didn't give a damn if they were living like neglected animals, as long as they got something like a day's work out of them.

You can't accuse the Derwent Valley Water Board of that sort of thing. It's bleak here, and I won't be sorry when we leave, though I suppose you have to admit that on a nice summer day, such as today, the hills look stunning.

That's if you've time to stand still and stare at them. But it's decent here, it's well run. You feel the bosses want to take a bit of care of you. And so they should, the work's hard enough, and dangerous too. That's why there's a hospital in the village, built specially for men who have accidents on the site, though it takes in the odd case from the families now as well. It sends a real chill down your spine when you hear a train coming this way from the dams, blowing its whistle in one long, hard blast - that's how they warn that a badly injured man is on his way in. Every time I hear it, I pray it's not George.

But this is the sort of place where you can give children a fair start in life. My three lads, Bob, young George and Walter, they've got a proper school to go to in the village. It's only a few strides from our front door, so there's no way they need to be led by the hand. Mr William Turner's the master, and his wife Elgiva, she's the school mistress. I've heard they're on a hundred and seventy-five pounds a year between them, which I happen to know is exactly the same as Mr and Mrs Upstone got at the Elan Valley school, seven years ago. I doubt if the Turners know that! You'd think they could have expected a bit more, especially as they've both been heads of other schools for years. At least the pair of them are very strict, and to my mind that's what it got to be, it's what children need, especially the ones from some of these families. Miss Sarah Eyre's got the youngest children, and she strikes me as being a bit too soft, but no doubt they all know Mr Turner's ready with his cane, if need be. There's a Mrs Edith Maude Kennedy there as well - Miss Hallett she was, until she married the local gamekeeper's son a couple of years back. Quite a posh wedding that was, but then her father's the foreman up at Howden site. He'll get paid a damn sight more than the workmen. The Turners don't do so badly, either - they get a much swankier hut than the rest of us. Three bedrooms and an inside lavatory! It would be my dream to have an inside lavatory.

At least we've got one we can call our own, out at the back of the hut. A proper draining lavatory too, not an earth closet. No sharing with other families, which I've had to do in my time. It's bad enough to be going out on a freezing winter's night, wrapped up in an old dressing-gown, without finding you've got to hang around and wait. Of course we use chamber pots at night when we can, and that's another job waiting to be seen to first thing in the morning, along with everything else. It wasn't at all easy when I was losing those two babies. Men just don't know what it is to have to cope with it all - the blood, the nasty smell, the feeling of always being in a horrible mess, to say nothing of the terrible pain. Thank God for that village bath house. They only charge tuppence, including a towel. At least I could escape up there once in a while, though of course I didn't dare to use their towels just then.

For once, George has got a Saturday afternoon off tomorrow. He wants us all to go and watch the football match, over on the Abbey Field. The team's making good use of the place, while it's still there. Once that lower dam - the Derwent - gets finished, it'll be under God knows how many feet of water. It's a good team this village has got, worth watching if you enjoy football, which I don't. But at least going out makes a bit of a change. Bob and young George get really excited now when they see the light blue shirts heading through the village, and they love being taken down to the rope footbridge across the river and onto the field. It would be a real relief if George would take the four of them, and give me a bit of peace. He probably would if I asked, he likes being with children more than I do. But I expect there'd be words said by some of those women, if they saw he'd been left to cope with a very young one. So no doubt I'll drag myself down there, and shout for the team with the rest of them.

Straight after the match, needless to say, the men will pour into that ale shop - the Derwent Canteen, it's called, but you'd be very lucky to find any food on offer. It's nothing but a drinking room for the workmen. The Temperance Society fought hard enough, in the early days, to ban all beer and spirits from the village, but the Water Board knew well enough how that would anger the men. They wouldn't have kept many of them for long. So the Board stuck out for the canteen and had it built just up from the railway line, with its own rolling way for the barrels, straight from the platform into the cellar. And they're probably right. All the men here do sweated labour and who's to say how they should spend their earnings or their bit of spare time? It's just a pity that some of them don't know when they've had enough. The first landlord of the place was thrown out of the door by a few of them, because he refused to serve a navvy that was already drunk. The one running it now, a Mr Mitchell, knows better than to try that. He goes along with things as they are.

There's no rule about women not going into that Canteen, in fact there's a bit of a side room where you can get soft drinks. But I don't know of many women that bother and I'm certainly not going near the place. If our team wins, you can be sure there'll be a lot of heavy drinking, and it's not unusual for a fight to break out when that happens. Not that fights seem to worry Neil MacLean, Birchinlee's policeman, (and he's another one that gets a better hut than the rest of us). MacLean has often taken a pair of fighters out of the canteen to some open space and told them to finish their quarrel off without putting anyone else in danger. I've even seen him wheel the loser home in a barrow before now! If that man was coming home to me, he'd get no sympathy. There'd be no soothing ointment in my hands.

George likes a drink, but he knows when enough's enough. Mind you, there can be a funny side to getting drunk. It's well known here that William Motley, who runs the greengrocer's shop, regularly drinks a lot more than he can take when he goes up to the market in Sheffield. If it wasn't for that horse of his - Dick it's called - he'd probably have been lying dead in some gutter over there long ago. The poor animal knows its own way back to this place - and I'm talking a good few miles, as you'll realise. It clops its way steadily home - full load of vegetables in the cart and its owner lying in the middle of it all - slumped out. We've had to throw water over his face to bring him round before now.

Last Saturday, there was a big dance in the Recreation Hall, with the usual whist drive beforehand. I like a game of whist and I've got a good mind for it. Would have suited me far better to play whist for the evening and hang the dance. Not that we stayed long anyway, not with the children in bed on their own. There's always a great many young women, from villages far and wide, turning out for those dances. No surprise, considering the number of single men in the lodging huts. It's quite obvious what those girls are after - same thing as I was at their age, and before. They're aiming to catch the eye of some young man with a good strong body and a bit of money to spend, and get him pinned down as quick as possible to a Sunday outing, an engagement, and as soon after that as they can manage it, a wedding. There's a fair few prepared to be willing enough beforehand as well, if they believe that's likely to hurry things along. It's a great pity they can't see their future life a bit more clearly - the endless making do, the daily round of cleaning and cooking, the long, dreary wash days. Within a few years they'll have the hands of an old woman. And then there's the man's rough ways - unless they're very lucky. If they could only see it all, then perhaps they'd be in a bit less of a hurry, and wouldn't think of it all as such a triumph.

At least we get cheap entertainment here, and more than enough of it. Not only dances and whist drives, but plenty of concerts and even cinema shows. And of course billiards, for the men. A lot of them would sooner be at that than spending time with their families. But people enjoying themselves isn't looked on by the church as some sinful affair, not like it often was in Wales, by those miserable-faced chapel ministers. In fact our village missioner, Mr George Sutton, usually comes to the events and has a chat with all sorts of people - not only about whether they attend services either, or when they're going to have their child christened. He's a nice man is Mr Sutton, very much on the serious side but a good man, who looks for good in other people. He's had his troubles too - wife died only three years back and he's been left with six children to care for. Little Fred was only two at the time. There's not many men in that position who wouldn't start scouting round pretty quick for a replacement, but not Mr Sutton. He's just got on with it. And he's not only here for the talk and the praying, either. He's got evening classes going in the village, and it's turned out there's plenty of people wanting to improve themselves.

Of course, Mr Sutton's not a proper minister, and this place hasn't got its own church. People can't get married here, although he's managed to get christenings brought to the village. They can use part of the school as a mission room. When those young women finally pin-down their navvy, they get themselves all dressed up to the nines and go along to the church in Derwent village. That church has held more weddings, christenings and funerals in the last few years than it probably did in the previous forty! But I'm quite sure the vicar won't have any complaints. I know for a fact he gets paid damn good money by the Water Board for taking on this village. He'll no doubt be heartily sorry when the place is pulled down.

Whether it's a wedding or a funeral, there's usually quite a tribe of people walking down to the church from here. I went along myself just a couple of weeks ago, and a very sad thing it was. Two babies buried on the same day, thirtieth of June. The Darkes' baby from hut 44, barely three weeks old, and then poor little Mary Stephens, just a day old, from hut 39. Both of them laid in the same grave. However often you know of young children dying, it's hard to see those tiny coffins being carried along the road. Felt a tear in my eye, and that's not something I'm prone to, not a bit. Life's something you just have to get on with, and I don't think any good comes of encouraging people to feel sorry for themselves. But I thanked God for little Violet that day. She's only fourteen months old, so not safe yet, not by any means. You can't really feel in the clear until at least the fifth year. But she looks strong and she's got a fighting spirit. You don't get by with anything less in this world.

At least there'll be a wedding to watch next month, Thomas Thorold and Gertrude Bean. She's twenty-one but he's a good ten years older, and a widower. Just hope she knows what she's about. No doubt they'll all be up to their usual tricks, tying ropes across the village road. The bride and groom won't be allowed to cross the ropes to get back to their hut until the best man hands over some coins at each one. Perhaps it's all done in a good spirit, but it can end up being costly for people. I wouldn't have found it at all funny myself.

I've just spotted John Townsend on the other side of the road - he'll be making his way across here any minute. The family are newsagents in Bamford, and John and his brother George bring papers up to Birchinlee every day on the train. The pair of them trundle round the village, though they're both as blind as bats! Amazing how they manage it. We get milk delivered too, from Crook Hill Farm and there's a few permanent shops here, as well as the mobile ones. Having mobile shops coming into the place means people can't push their prices up too high, which is what they do the minute there's no competition. No good relying on anyone's sense of decency. We get a horse-drawn fish-and-chip cart up from Sheffield once a week - it's the lads' favourite, that one, not that they get it every time. I'd rather buy a few ends of raw fish myself and some proper potatoes - that is when Sam Somersett's not too drunk to manage his fish cart. He ran it right off the road a couple of weeks back. Straight down the bank it went and of course turned upside down, fish thrown around everywhere. He had to sell them off cheap that day, and serves him right

George is hoping to be driving one of the work's engines before too long, which should mean just a bit more money to go round. There's a railway line comes from the quarry at Grindleford, with all the stone needed to build these dams. It goes into the Waterworks Sidings near Bamford station and from there a line comes up to this site, specially laid for the job. It doesn't only carry stone, it brings wood, coal and anything else the village needs. Takes a good few local workmen up to the dams as well. We've got a platform at Birchinlee and any of us in the village can travel on the train free, as long as we get a pass. I've no doubt they'll have picked George out as having a good bit more about him than most, that's why he was moved up a while back, from general digging to operating a crane. There's plenty of them that stay on the digging for their entire lives.

"Just you wait till I'm driving that engine," he says to me. "I'll give the lads a ride on the footplate... and little Violet too."

"You'll not be taking her for a good while yet!" I barks back at him.

"She'll be safe," he says, "I'd not let her come to any harm."

He wouldn't either. I don't need telling that I've been lucky. He's a good father to the lot of them, and no doubt he'll carry on being good to any others that arrive. Much as I'd like to think she was the last, it's too much to hope that she will be. It's going to be a while yet before I can say goodbye to all of that. To be honest, it'll come as a great relief to be rid of the whole shenanigans - the bearing of them, all those years of rearing, even the means of getting them in the first place! I've got to admit that I sometimes dream of a very different sort of life, but I know now I'm never going to have it. "Once you've made your bed..." as my Mam always enjoyed warning me.

That big Yates family, down at hut 23, are talking about going off to live in New Zealand next year. Are there really places like this on the other side of the world? What a strange thought. "We're going to give the children a better chance in life," so Grace Yates has told me.

Sometimes I feel I could take a risk like that. After all, what's to lose? But I know very well that George wouldn't. He's a very contented man. He's fond of his comrades, he's at ease in the village, he even enjoys his work. So we're here till the job ends, and after that who knows? No doubt it'll be on to the next big project, the next huge building site, another tin hut.

I just hope when our Violet stands on that footplate, smells the hissing steam and feels the engine get up speed, that she looks out at the world around her, and lifts her hopes up a bit higher than mine.

Professor Brian Robinson's mother, Violet Mary Green, as an infant with her younger sister, Lilian, inside their home at hut number 52 in Birchinlee.

Historical Note

Between 1901 and 1914, a village existed on the west side of the Upper Derwent Valley, close to what is now the edge of the Derwent Resevoir. This village was built for nomadic workers (navvies) and their families, and was made up of wooden buildings, covered with corrugated iron. That accounts for its nickname of 'Tin Town', though the correct name was Birchinlee.

All the men of Birchinlee were engaged on a massive project - the construction of Howden and Derwent Dams and the creation of their two great reservoirs. (Ladybower Resevoir did not come into existence until much later).

At a time when navvies often lived in appalling conditions, the standard of provision here was high. However, the work could be dangerous (eighteen men were killed during construction) and labourers were not protected by the safety regulations of today. Helmets were never worn, even when working underground or with cranes lifting huge slabs of stone, and machinery was uncovered. An accident hospital in the village was therefore essential.

I was moved to write 'A View from the Hut' through the friendship of Prof. Brian Robinson, whose mother was born in Birchinlee. Brian has written several scholarly books about both the village itself and the construction of the dams, and has kindly given permission for the photographs here to be used.

It has been fascinating to talk to Brian about his mother, Violet, his grandmother, Molly, and his navvy grandfather, 'Long' George Green (he was some six feet and six inches tall). This tale is told by Molly, and I have tried to convey the discontented but very tough character she is remembered as! Others, who are mentioned by Molly in her tale, were of course all real people of Birchinlee.

Exm.
Riley Graves.

R.P. 2006,

The Plague Woman's Tale

Does our village look lovely to you now? How quaint, how idyllic! Charming even on a damp and overcast day. Some of you no doubt believe that you would like to live in such a place, perhaps raise young children here, or find in it a retreat for old age? It is heavy with memories, preserved almost perfectly in time, holding the essence of Old England.

But be thankful that your eyes never opened upon this village when I, as a young woman, lived here. Looking back upon my childhood I remember it fondly, as a place filled with down to earth people of character, of toughness, of generosity. Yet it was hard and unyielding, a windswept cluster of homes surrounded by desolate hills, where the weather was so often harsh, where earning the means of survival was a demanding task, faced grindingly each day. In the steep sloping fields where I often toiled as a girl, or in the watery gloom of the lead mine where Thomas laboured, life offered nothing of ease or comfort.

Yet how much more we might have treasured our simple means of survival, our youth, our health, had we glimpsed what was to come.

As I approached the age of nineteen and Thomas reached twenty, God began to punish our village for what surely must have been some terrible sins. It began abruptly, and it was Thomas himself who brought me the first piece of news. After his usual labours (never would I have exchanged the chill open fields for those dank caverns) he came, as so often, to our small and slightly crumbling farmhouse for some broth. The word 'farmhouse' exaggerates its size. It was, like many others, but a substantial cottage at the edge of a few acres of smallholding, a little under a mile from the village centre. This distance, often seeming inconvenient to me as a child, was probably to prove my salvation, and that of my father. My mother had died in childbirth some six years before, taking with her my infant brother, and I had long been expected, as the only daughter, to occupy her place in all matters of housekeeping. My help was required in no less a measure outside, where hens, ducks, a few sheep and a crop of oats provided scantily for most of our needs. In his own interest, father would probably have preferred me never to marry. Nevertheless he seemed to like Thomas, to whom I had promised my hand, and made him as welcome as his own taciturn soul would allow. Thomas was far stronger and abler than my brother, two years my senior, and a reliable source of practical help when the elements turned viciously against us.

That evening, early in September 1665 (how could the season, the year, not be etched deep into my memory?) Thomas told us that George Viccars was dead. I should explain to you that George was a tailor, who seemed to have travelled quite widely in the country and who had for some time been lodging with Mary Cooper - once a close friend of my mother - in her cottage at the heart of the village. Faces changed little at that time, and a stranger's face was always an object of curiosity. Many had made themselves acquainted with George, had been fascinated by his travels. He had connections with the London cloth trade, a fact that was to prove the trap door through which we would fall to our misery. Only later was this known, of course. Only later were stories passed around that cloth he had received in a box from that city, which was hung on a rail to air, was the carrier of disease.

Naturally there was sorrow at the news of his death, which had apparently happened quickly, following a brief but violent illness. George had endured a raging fever, had screamed at the pain in his head. His body had been shaking uncontrollably and bathed in foul smelling sweat. Beneath his arms strange and grossly engorged lumps had suddenly appeared, a livid red colour.

Such ills were not unheard of by certain older members of our community. Despite this and the whispered horror of his state, we were as yet unsuspecting of what was to come.

Within no less than a few days, three of George's neighbours were dead, each of them suffering the same bodily agonies as he himself had endured. Fear began to spread through the people of our village as we sensed a growing, malign danger to us all. My father, with an instinctive wisdom, bade me stay within the confines of our house and its fields. I did not long do so. Just sixteen days later, in early October, I heard that a childhood friend lay dying. As I stood at the doorway of her stench filled room, uttering a prayer with her distraught mother, I begged God to have mercy on her, and upon us all.

No fewer than twenty-three people of our village died that month. Mary Cooper's three year old son, Edward, was amongst them and her five year old Jonathon was lost to her just ten days later. How she must have cursed the day she took a lodger into her home! Grief and terror were now in the very air we breathed. My father did not forbid Thomas to visit us and he came each evening, so that we both might be reassured of the other's continuing good health. Daily now we became aware of new illness, of rapid death, of hysterical scenes of grief. No longer did we talk of our future, our marriage, but only grasped at the presence of each other in that moment.

Those who were able were already leaving this place of disease and death. Their number included, unsurprisingly, the land owning Sheldons, the family of Bradshaw Hall and others whose means afforded them some independence of action. Most of us had nowhere to go, no easy means of earning a living beyond our village and its farmland, where almost all had lived from birth. My father did not even consider such a solution. A deeply religious and inward looking man, he held little fear of death and believed we should continue to work, to pray, to put our trust in God and take what fate awaited us. Thomas had cousins in Baslow and could perhaps have gone to them. He did not. For this I have felt a heavy burden of guilt throughout my life.

I now know that our village was not unique in its suffering. Over the years, other villages and many towns had been similarly visited. But as grief and panic engulfed us, our people took actions that were special, indeed that were, as far as I am aware, unknown before or since. If you suspect we did so because we were people of special courage, you would be quite wrong. We did this because we had living in the village two men of quite exceptional character.

Mr Mompesson was our church minister, stricken by what he was witnessing around him, desperately anxious for the safety of his wife and young children. I was told he begged Catherine to leave. She would not, but finally agreed to send the children to safety in north Yorkshire. She remained with him, supporting and comforting the sick and bereaved, especially the children who could not, unlike her own, be sent to safety.

Her husband, however, sensed that more was needed than acts of mercy, that far more was demanded than prayer. Whether God moved within him I do not know. At that time he was quite a young man, not yet thirty, in addition to being fairly new to our parish. He was not therefore a natural leader for us during this terrifying time. Mercifully he was helped and guided by the previous incumbent, the Puritan minister Mr Stanley, who was at that time living in the village. The two now knew it was vital to bury the differences of religious view which had previously divided them so deeply, to speak to us with one voice.

In the June of that terrible year of 1666, these two men faced the people of the village together. They had decided on a course of action, one that was not intended to save us, indeed one which would make us all prisoners within this pit of disease. What we heard from their mouths was hard indeed. What they asked of us was more than should be demanded of simple people.

Until such time as God lifted this terrible curse from us, no person would move beyond agreed village boundaries (within which my own dwelling lay). We would no longer gather in large groups, which risked further spread of disease. Therefore, from that day, the church would be locked and no further funerals would take place. Families and neighbours must bury the dead, as quickly as possible after their demise and at good depth.

There was, of course, deep distress at such suggestions. Most had not the means of fleeing, yet cherished their freedom to do so. To bury loved ones without church ceremony, to cast them hastily into makeshift graves, was horrifying to religious minds. There was deep concern also about the wherewithal of our survival, even if such survival was to be temporary. The village was not self-supporting, its appalling death toll making it less so as each day passed. How would we be fed? This vital question, however, had already been considered by the two gentlemen, who had called upon the generosity of the Duke at Chatsworth. Food and other essentials could be brought for us and left at certain agreed points along our outer boundaries.

To provide comfort and mutual support, a religious service would be held weekly in the open. The place chosen for this was the Delph, a large but enclosed 'basin' close to the village centre where some form of collective worship could take place, but in which families would be able to stand well apart. All of us would undertake to remain in this village, to be its willing prisoners. By doing this we would perhaps safeguard the lives of others beyond our boundaries. We would be doing a Holy thing. We would be Blessed.

There was much anguish. There was some anger. There were tears and there was blaspheming. But finally we agreed.

Confinement within our own boundaries began at once. Rules were abided by in almost all respects, but we were human. Some of us were young, and felt the terror of both life and love being ripped from us. Another childhood friend of mine, Emmot Sidall, had planned to marry a young man in the neighbouring village of Stony Middleton. Throughout that terrible winter of 1665 to 1666 he had come each day to the village to ensure that she was well. Finally, she begged him not to endanger his life anymore. However, unbeknown to Emmot's widowed mother, who had lost her husband and five children by the end of 1665, the couple continued to meet on occasions in the more sheltered fringes of the Delph. But the birth of spring was cruel. The poor girl fell ill and died towards the end of April and Rowland waited for her many times in vain. It appears that no-one let him know, but in the horror of that time people faced grief and loss on every side and all of us were stricken. Emmot's mother, Elizabeth, had remarried just five days before Emmot was so cruelly taken. Sadly, her new husband was to follow his stepdaughter to the grave in July.

I know that Rowland was one of the first to enter the village when the curse of disease was finally lifted from us. He must in his heart have known what news awaited him, but it seems he had not quite extinguished hope.

As midsummer of 1666 approached, death gathered pace and strength. Neither youth nor health offered any protection and those of us who remained well grew more certain each day that we too must finally be doomed. My brother, always lazy and inadequate, became more so, offering precious little help on the farm, retreating into solitude and stupor. Against my father's will, he drank with the owners of the Miners Arms, an inn no longer used by the villagers.

Was it there that the hand of death touched his shoulder? We buried him two days after that first fever, my father and Thomas dragging his blackening corpse, wrapped in an old sheet, to the furthest corner of our land. I wept, but my grief was small against that which ravaged me just three weeks later.

Thomas failed to appear at the farm around his usual hour. Aware that he had seemed exhausted the previous day, and had barely eaten, I was thrown into panic. Rushing down towards the far side of the village, I entered the worker's cottage he shared with his widowed mother. I found her struck silent, motionless, suffering a grief too great for her mind to bear. Thomas had fallen ill the previous evening, not two hours after leaving me. Throughout the night, his mother later told me, she had tried to minister to his unquenchable thirst, to wipe the blood seeping from his nostrils and mouth, to calm his delirious ramblings. Death had taken him with even more savage speed than was usual and he had died just after midday.

Already her neighbours had dragged his still warm body up the rough track beside the cottage and had buried it in the oat field beyond. She could not walk there with me. I walked alone. Standing by the rough overturned earth, I thanked God that his suffering had not been prolonged.

Grieving was the normality of my life and of the lives of everyone around me. No longer did any horror shock. When I heard that Mrs Hancock, a good, kind woman, had lost her husband and her five children, and that the sixth lay dying, I remained almost unmoved, quite unable to shed a tear, too numbed to utter a prayer. Perhaps such numbness is God's way of preserving us against what might otherwise overwhelm and destroy. Mrs Hancock, who lived at the eastern end of the village, dragged each one of her family from her home to a nearby place, a bleak hillside spot known as Riley. Within a mere six days all seven had died and had been roughly, unceremoniously buried by her own poor hands. I believe she then fled in her grief to Sheffield, to spend the rest of her days with her one remaining son, who worked there in the cutlery trade. Surely no one could condemn such an escape? Only now do I see clearly the horrors God willed her to endure.

She was, nonetheless, luckier in her flight than another, a desperate woman who tried to flee unnoticed to Tideswell, on that town's market day. She was pelted with stones and driven back by terrified villagers, then to face the anger and scorn of our own people.

I no longer even attempted to confine myself to the farm, but used my energies to be of practical help to others. Often I walked to one boundary point or another to collect the provisions generously left there (though no doubt it was a price others felt to be worth paying, in exchange for our isolation). For certain things, such as materials, coins needed to be passed across. These I would drop into a small hole, gouged into the surface of the boundary stone and filled with cleansing vinegar.

We came to respect our minister increasingly, all the more so after his wife's death in mid-summer. His obvious grief did not long deter him from his tasks of comfort, support, of organisation. Those of us who lived did not go hungry and we were not let down by the ones who had promised him to supply us with food. I understand that much later, and in another place, he married once again and I hope that he was rewarded with happiness.

In the autumn of that terrible year of 1666, God decided we had endured enough. Whatever evil had been done in this place, we had paid for it with our suffering. It seems now that the last death from this terrible curse took place on the first day of November, though naturally we did not realise this to be the case until much later. August and September had been terrible, cruel months with more than a hundred deaths. The fall to fourteen deaths in October had raised our hope only slightly. Such hope had been raised, and cruelly dashed, before.

Slowly, as November progressed into deep winter, I allowed myself to believe I might survive. For many though, the mere fact of survival was not cause for joy or celebration. Some had lost every person they had ever loved and older people, in particular, knew they would never recover. Their losses were too savagely complete. But, gradually and fearfully, others appeared in this place, usually seeking news of a distant relative.

Mr Mompesson, in his wisdom, encouraged us all to burn our clothes, our furniture and bedding, and huge bonfires could regularly be seen in and around the village. Perhaps we should have made fires earlier. Perhaps we should have destroyed our very homes, and lived, as indeed a few did, in simple huts on the hills.

Be that as it may, some accumulation of pain was now eased in the lighting of fires, in the crackling sounds of hungry flames. The few remaining young started to grasp at excitement once again. Life will not for too long be held down.

This tale has gone on long enough. Take a walk around our village and beyond. Visit the beautiful church, once locked to us. Look at the cottages, such appealing places, once the containers of pain, of fear, of death. Visit the simple graves of poor Mrs Hancock's family, just a few graves among so very many, most of the others unmarked. If you decide to walk as far as Stony Middleton, think of Emmot and Rowland, of their sad love. By our actions, I believe we saved the lives of those who lived in that place, whose boundary lies so close to our own.

There are beautiful and interesting things to see as you walk, far more than I have been able to mention. Enjoy them......... and be grateful!

EYAM
STOCKS

Historical Note

Eyam is famous as the 'Plague Village', attracting many visitors every year for that reason. There are a number of information plaques along the village's High Street, lots more detail in its lovely church, and a small museum devoted largely to the history of the Plague.

Plague was common throughout Europe from the 14th century onwards, and there were few towns in England that did not suffer at some time, and often repeatedly. What made Eyam so special was the decision of the villagers to isolate themselves totally from the outside world, in an attempt to prevent the disease spreading into surrounding areas.

The horrifying and virulent Bubonic Plague ('Black Death') hit London in 1665. It brought rapid and painful death, preceded by hugely swollen glands (buboes), fever, vomiting, splitting headache, swollen tongue and terrible thirst. It was this which some believe to have reached Eyam, transported by fleas infesting a box of cloth sent to the village tailor.

Although this view is still held, it has been disputed by several well-qualified authorities, who suggest that the village may well have succumbed to some other form of illness. Infected fleas could not have survived the long journey from London, it is claimed. Nor, it has been argued, would the villagers' voluntary isolation have protected neighbouring places, as it appeared to do. Black rats and their fleas, known to be the main spreaders of Bubonic Plague, would certainly not have confined themselves within village boundaries!

Whatever the truth, an epidemic of some form swept through the village of Eyam in 1665 and 1666, presenting some similar symptoms to those above and killing two hundred and sixty people, from seventy-six families. The people of Eyam acted in a way that was selfless and courageous and it this which has given them their lasting place in Derbyshire's history.

Letter from the Quarryman

Derwent Valley Water Board
Bole Hill Quarry Site
Nr. Grindleford
Derbyshire
13th February 1903

Dear Ma

Don't drop dead at the shock! This is me, your long lost son, the boy you last set eyes on three years ago - or is it more? Not penned by me, of course. That'd take a bit more schooling than I've had. You're getting this letter thanks to a Mr Pritchard, a gentleman from Wales who's taken me in as one of his lodgers. I'm talking him through it now, him and me sitting at the big table in his living room, a paraffin lamp hanging over us, though he could do with it being a bit brighter. He's found us some decent paper from somewhere - it's not something I often need. And he's been saying for a long time that I should put your mind at rest, before it's too late and perhaps I'll get news that your whole body's been laid down to rest. If that was to happen, so he tells me, I'd never forgive myself. Well, maybe I wouldn't, though I'm not one who feels I owe anyone anything. Nothing's ever come to me on a plate. Still, here's hoping this finds you well. You could even try to send me a line back, if you feel the urge to. First time in years I've had something called an address.

Can see you in my mind, going down the street to Aunt Bessie's when you get this, telling her to read it out, that's if she's got any sight left. It'll probably surprise her that I'm not in prison somewhere.

Must be about as far as I've ever been from you, Ma. Up in Derbyshire, near some place called Grindleford, not that it's worth spitting for. Nearest real town is Sheffield, and a good number of men come in every day from there. By *in* I mean to this quarry - that's the work I'm on. But just saying quarry can't tell you what this place is like. I've worked in a couple of others over the last few months, but they were nothing against this one.

We're getting stone out of here to build two hulking great dams - they're going to fill up a whole valley a few miles away - the Derwent Valley, it's called. It'll take years to build them - which is all to the good as far as I'm concerned - and when they're done they'll hold enough water for half the country, by the sound of it.

Could have worked right there, right on the dams. That's where I first landed up after I walked out of the last job. Took me long enough to get there, just on something I'd heard, not knowing if I was sure of work at the end of it. Couldn't believe my eyes - nothing like any of the dumps I'd worked at before. Usually you're lucky if there's as much as a leaking shed roof over your head. At most places there's men sleeping out in old tents, or else they're under hedges, in hen houses, just about anywhere. Last place I was, one of the older men died in the night. Nothing wrong that you could see, just cold, hungry, living a hard life for too long. Nobody in charge gave a toss. But at these dams there's a proper set up, what you'd call a sort of navvy village. There's rows of houses, a canteen, a few shops, the lot. Even a little hospital! Youngsters all round the place too, and they've got proper schoolrooms for them there. Tin Town, they call it, because the houses are made of corrugated iron on the outside. Well, I knew right away that I'd stay there a while if I got the chance, if nothing else just to get into a proper bed for a bit. They told me I was to sleep over at the doss house for the first night. That's the rule, and if you don't get an offer of work the next day, you've got to move on. That'd have been a big blow. Just as well I'd got enough on me to pay for the night - sixpence it cost me.

It was all right, that doss house - a bed to myself, clean sheets, clean night-shirt. First rule is - you take a bath, and when I was sitting there in it, scrubbing myself down, this woman (sort of female you don't argue with) put my clothes in a sack and made off with them. That got me worried! Only had what I'd stood up in. Got them back next morning - stank of disinfectant, but not so much of grime and sweat.

Anyway, there was even a good bit of bacon for breakfast, and then a while later one of the bosses had a word with me. Pricked his ears up when I told him about the quarrying I'd done. Said they needed a few more men up at Bole Hill - that's this place - and would I be willing to work on that end of things? Told me there were huts to lodge in up here, just like the ones I'd already seen. Said to him I wasn't bothered, just so long as I had a bed to lie in and some paid work. And that was that. By the rules, I should have stayed in that doss house for a full week, just in case I was carrying smallpox or something. But he said I looked well enough and he didn't seem to want any hanging around. Told me he could see I had a look in my eye, and a mouth on me, and he warned me to keep it shut. Rules were strict, he said, there was to be no answering back, no fighting, no getting drunk just before a shift. I said I'd manage that, for as long as it suited me. So he got me up here on the train that morning, and I was put on to work next day.

This place looks just like ants swarming over an ant hill - must be around four hundred men - and there's rock faces being worked all over the hillside, and further. They've put down tracks, so engines and wagons can get along the ledges underneath rock faces, and you can see great lifting cranes everywhere, bringing down huge blocks to be put on the wagons. Nearly thirty tons each, they weigh. Mostly I'm working at the foot of a face, helping to get blocks off a crane, knocking rough ends off with a pick, making sure they're good enough for putting into the walls of those two dams. The rock's about as hard as you'll ever get. Gritstone, it's called, and it can be a real devil to work on, takes a strong man to do it. Even needs explosives, sometimes, to loosen it out of the face. And I'm told there's more than two million tons of the stuff here. We get about six thousand tons a week out if there's no hold ups. Thing is, whole lot's got to be pushed three hundred feet down a very steep hill, to get it to the main railway line below - that's the railway that takes it off to the dams. There's a great winding drum at the top of the hill, turning a cable, and the trick is that an empty wagon coming up lets a full one go down. Scares you when you first set eyes on it. Operated by a brake-man called Tom Green and I wouldn't mind being put on it if he ever goes, but I don't suppose it's ever likely to come my way.

Anyway, you're probably not too bothered about all that. Don't know what you're bothered about, Ma, to be truthful, except where the next penny's coming from. Now that I've got myself together a bit, I'll try and send you a pound or two from time to time. Wages aren't bad here - sevenpence ha'penny an hour, though there's a lot that think we should be on at least a penny more. Talk is that we'll be out on strike for it by next month.

Course I have to pay for food, which isn't cheap here, though it's not the swindling price they charge at a lot of sites. And I give Mr P a fair bit for my lodging. There's four of us at the moment sleeping in his lodgers' room, but faces have changed a bit over the months. Rules are too strict here for some, they can't take it, or they can't keep off the drink. Mr and Mrs P have a bedroom, and then there's this living room for the whole lot of us, though we're on our own in here just now. Others are across in one of the mess rooms, playing cards. There's a cooking range in here, I can throw some bacon or something on it and brew a pot of tea, but Mrs P quite often cooks stew and dumplings and then we'll all sit round of an evening. Other huts are nearly all just for working men. It's not families here, not like at Tin Town. Place is always kept clean though, but they still inspect it once a week to make sure.

We've got no hospital or school at Bole Hill. No children around here, and that's good, because they can get on your nerves. If there's an accident, a doctor comes in from a place called Hathersage - bit bigger than Grindleford but still nothing much. Takes him a while to get here, which isn't funny if it's a bad injury. He had to come up yesterday, as a matter of fact. There was a nasty accident, and to be honest that's what's got me round to writing to you, that and Mr P's nagging. Afternoon, it was, but in fact there'd already been an accident in the morning. It's not as if this is a bad place to work either, not like a lot of sites where there's men getting injured, or worse, by the day. No end of rules here - machines checked every day, no one allowed to work if they're the worse for drink. It's not a place for anyone soft, that I can tell you, but it's about as safe as you'll get in this way of work.

But early on yesterday, couple of men got injured - pushed down from a rock face by a stone that'd worked loose from a crane. Bit messed up they are - one's had all his ribs crushed - but from what I've heard it could have been worse. Shook me up a bit though - I wasn't far off when they fell - but not nearly so bad as in the afternoon, when I heard what'd happened to Will. Bit daft, Will, bit of a simpleton. Came in from Hathersage every day and he'd been working with me on the same face for a good while. Few years older than me, about middle twenties. Took him under my wing a bit, don't know why. Not often I bother about anyone else, my own fights are more than enough, I don't choose to take on other people's. But for some reason I kept an eye out for Will, made sure the others didn't yell at him too much for being slow, gave him a hand now and then. Anyway, yesterday afternoon he wasn't up on the face with me, he was at the bottom of the slope, though I still don't know why. Three wagons broke loose from the cable halfway up the hill and went crashing down the line. A lot of us heard yelling and shouting from down there, but then there's always a lot of noise around. Will was a bit deaf, but maybe if he'd been brighter he'd have got away in time. Hit full on, he was, flesh and blood all over the lines. No point in getting Dr Lander out, nothing anyone could do for him. He's been taken off to lie at the Millstone Inn just down the road, what was still in one piece that is, and there's going to be some fuss about it because it should never have happened. Upset a lot of men, it did, even though they'd seen a good many accidents in their time. That's why Mr P said it would do me good to write this letter to you.

Anyway Ma, Mr P's looking tired now. It's taken us a few hours to pen this, and that's after we've done a full day's labour. He's good to do this for me, can't ever remember anyone taking trouble for me like he does. Almost like having a dad, not that I'd know. It'll be a while before you're likely to see me at the door again, though I don't fool myself that me being a long way off gives you much grief. Going to stay here as long as it lasts, or at least as long as I can hold that temper of mine in and not land myself in trouble. Better chance of that now than there was before. I might even keep my eyes open for a girl up here. You'd be surprised if you saw me - don't look at all bad when I'm scrubbed up and I'm not short of a bit of muscle. A lot of girls like that, especially if you've got a bob or two to spend on them. First time I've ever had a bit to spare. There's a few of the men taken up with local girls. Had their fill of moving all over the country, from one dump to another.

Can't think what on earth this place will look like when we're through with the stone, when it's all packed up and we're gone. Won't be for a long while, of course. Whole hill's been torn apart, you can't think that anything green will ever grow on it again. Not that it worries me, plenty of other hills around here.

Look after yourself, Ma.

Frank

Historical Note

In 1901, Parliament authorised the building of the Howden and Derwent Dams. As well as a massive workforce, this project required, of course, enormous amounts of stone. Where could such a vast quantity of high quality stone be found?

The answer - after much dispute - was Bole Hill, just outside Grindleford, close to Padley Gorge. In November 1901, the Derwent Valley Water Board bought its fifty-two acres, harbouring almost two and a half million tons of millstone grit. Work began immediately, and in earnest.

The young navvy, Frank, who writes here to his mother, is one of over four hundred quarrymen at Bole Hill. The work must have been tough, as millstone grit (or gritstone) becomes very hard and unyielding, where it has been exposed to the weather. Lack of safety regulations meant that accidents were common, though only two fatal events occurred in this quarry. One of these - causing the death of Will - is spoken of in Frank's letter.

Frank is a lodger in a workman's hut. These huts were similar to those at Birchinlee, the 'navvy village' built near Howden Dam. However, the set up at Bole Hill was more basic, as it was labourers, rather than whole families, catered for here. Many navvies married local girls and settled in the area, giving up their previously nomadic way of life.

It is fascinating to walk up Bole Hill, to look at the steep incline - down which wagons of stone had to be lowered - and the old quarry faces. Everything is now so green and overgrown that it is hard to picture the noisy, industrial scene it once was!

The Marble Man's Tale

The candle's not got long to go now. It was a nasty thing, giving off the evil smell of pig tallow. The air in the shed is stuffy, but cold. I shall be glad enough to get inside the house, have some beer and a plate of hot stew. Working days have been long of late, longer than ever.

"This stuff needs to be good," so the man in Matlock Bath has told me. "It must be of the very best," he says, "if I'm to take it to London for that exhibition in the Crystal Palace." Well, I pride myself that my work is as good as any in Ashford - why else would he keep buying bits from me, to sell in what he calls his museum? But if it's taken to London, then who knows? Please God it might put more meat on the table, even give us a little to put by in case times get harder.

Alice should have got the young ones to bed by now - six of them, if you count James, though at twelve he's not really young any more. Of course they won't be asleep, there'll be a din going on in that room up there, and I'll be expected to bellow up the staircase and make sure it stops - or else. Can't blame them, but you've got to be hard with children or they'll run all over you. Alice is heavy and exhausted, she hasn't been well from the start this time, in fact the sooner it's born the better. And if I could have my wish, then this would be the last one. There's plenty of folk around with more, but seven hungry bellies are enough for me, and enough for Alice, what with the two she lost a few years back. Of course it'll be eight in all, but Clara went into service earlier this year when she reached fourteen, up at Thornbridge Hall, and very lucky she was to be taken in there. Not many village girls get such a chance, but then Clara is more polite and tidier looking than most. She wasn't too happy about going, and nor was Alice, but I was firm. "She'll get three decent meals a day there," I said, "and the chance to learn some respectable ways. She might even marry something a bit better than what you see around the village." And of course, it's one less mouth to feed.

Don't misunderstand me, the children get as much food as there is going. There's many a time I've taken less than I had the appetite for, so they wouldn't go hungry. Since my sister Sarah lost her two oldest, I suppose

I've had an even greater care for my own. Two healthy strong boys, eight and ten years they were, fell down an old mineshaft a few months back, while out larking around. Bodies not found for days on end. You can imagine what it was like. She even lost the one she was carrying, in all that grief. The whole village was out for the funerals of course, as it usually is. There's some that want to grieve with you, there's some that want to pray it won't happen to them, and there's some that just enjoy the spectacle - whether it's of joy or grief. They weren't the first to be killed by falling down a shaft, far from it. There's been more than a small number over the last few years, and not just around this village either. Those hills are death traps, it's time that they did something to stop it. It's surely not impossible to cover the damn holes up! But then, it's not the children of the rich getting killed, is it? They're not left out to roam around, are they? Couldn't keep mine shut up inside - we'd all go mad, or else I'd probably kill them. One living room, that's what we have, the one with the range. There's a little front room, but Alice makes sure that's kept nice for Sundays, and then only for her and myself, and the odd visitor. Otherwise it wouldn't be nice for long, would it? It's her one pride and joy, that room, especially the corner cabinet with a couple of bits of china her mother passed on to her when we got married. Fifteen years ago that, spring of 1836. We didn't marry until she was pregnant with Clara. That might surprise you, but lots of country folk don't marry until there's the first on its way. It's easier for a single girl to get proper work, and it's best to hold on to that for as long as you can. Alice used to work a stocking frame up the village - four or five lasses in a workshop upstairs. Mind you, there wasn't much future left in it. It went years ago, all that kind of trade has moved to bigger places now, into factories nearer the towns.

Alice's older sister even suggested she should get rid of the baby. "You're only eighteen," she said, "you've plenty of time yet," and offered to get her a tot of turpentine. Alice didn't drink it though. She was already living with me here, it was my father's cottage then, and she knew I'd marry her. Just as well I did, because she nursed him through that terrible time before he died, weaker than a new born babe, not able to raise a spoon to his mouth or put one shaking foot to the floor. That's thirty years of lead mining for you. He was forty-five years old and he'd had a longer life than a good many of those that worked alongside him.

Of course, I should have been a miner myself. The family hasn't known much else other than its menfolk working the mines. Three older brothers were at the Magpie, out near Sheldon, a wretched place, always flooding. The oldest was drowned down there, and the mine has lost many a man that way or crushed under falling rocks. There's some folk believe there must be a curse on that place. Of course lead mining's on the wane now and there's plenty of men out of work, lots of children not getting the food they need. The Magpie's even had to close at times, and then the two of them have been out looking for something else. William wanted to join up with me a while back. "We could make this business bigger," he says, "build a proper workshop, make more stuff, sell it all ourselves." He thinks that black marble's here to stay, that the price will keep going up.

The trouble is, William just hasn't got the skill in his hands, never could have. After all the years of rough work he's done, his hands are like great red shovels. I doubt if there's an ounce of sensitive flesh in his fingertips. If you pushed a pin into them, I'd be surprised if he so much as noticed it. It's just not a skill he could be taught, and in any case those huge hands would never be steady enough, because like most miners he's very fond of his beer. They say it protects them from being poisoned by the lead, that's what I'm often told, but I've got my doubts. In any case I'm someone who likes to work on my own. The shed's small, you can barely call it a workshop, but when I'm in here chipping away at the marble, forming the white jasmine flowers that I've made a bit of a speciality of, I'm my own man and I'm answerable to no one else.

Of course it's not really marble, it's limestone of a type you can polish up until it's jet black, smooth and gleaming, like nothing else you'll ever see. His Grace the Duke, at Chatsworth, has got a good bit of it around his house, and the Queen herself bought a table of it a few years back. Of recent times it's the pretty designs inlaid in it that make black marble so special, the flowers, the leaves. Those of us with the skill to do it often favour a particular bloom, and we pride ourselves in creating a true representation, as well as a beautiful one. When I look at the white flowers of my jasmine, the bend of the green leaves, all laid into the shining black surface as if they'd been formed there, I get a real pride. Rub your finger over the surface and you feel no join, no line, nothing. That's the real skill, you see, but it takes years to perfect, and the doing of it is hard and painstaking. Most days I've a badly aching back from sitting on this stool, a brooch or a small vase or some such article held between my knees, bending over it for hours on end. Those of us that earn our living this way are often called 'baublers', an insult if ever there was one. The things we

65

make are of great beauty, trinkets or baubles they are most certainly not. Trinkets cost a lot less for a start. I gave a little brooch to Clara when she went up to the hall, just a simple oval thing with a tiny white flower. She wears it for church and it's already been much admired, so I gather. There may even be an order or two coming from up there, I certainly hope so.

I have to make small things here, there isn't the space for doing tables and the like. And anyway, I wouldn't want to put all my efforts for too long into one large object. It might make a lot more money, but if things go wrong towards the end, it's a lot more lost, isn't it? I couldn't afford to contemplate that. So I keep to brooches and pendants and small plates and vases. Sometimes visitors to the village buy from our door - I always keep a few bits in the window of the front room. And of course occasionally the man with the museum in Matlock Bath comes and buys quite a few objects, and orders yet more. He sells a lot in his museum, it's a shop by another name, where people who come up to take the spa waters can wander around and admire. He buys from all over the place, so he tells me, as far as Buxton and Derby. But he certainly seems to like what I do here, and if I did as William has suggested, expand things, perhaps take a lad on to train, then maybe I'd make a fair bit more. But as I said, I like my own company, I don't want to be at anyone's beck and call, and my needs are few. The children are fed well enough, mainly on Alice's turnip and carrot stew, which she seems to have simmering most of the day on the range, stocked up from the supply of vegetables under our bed. There's nowhere else to keep them and anyway it's dark under there and fewer mice around than downstairs. I like stew best when it's got some pork in it, and it sometimes has on account of the old sow we keep out in the back. She's been a good breeder, it's worth paying the farmer for the use of his boar occasionally. Teaches the young ones a bit about life at the same time, because those beasts don't exactly go about things quietly. It was an eye opener to me as a young lad, and it saved my father, who wouldn't have known what words to say to me, from ever having to open his mouth. Saves me the same thing, and there's no better teacher than nature.

Of course there's not a lot left over from our plates to feed the sow on. The children learnt early on that if they don't eat what's on the table, then there's nothing else. But she gets the scrapings of the pot, as well as peelings and any windfall crabby apples or acorns that the children can find. Anyway she seems to produce good young that fatten up well. It's the fat you want of course, it sticks to the chest much better than lean, especially in winter.

I like beer with a meal if there's any going, though I don't personally frequent the village alehouses - rough places they are, often open till the early hours of the morning. Alice sometimes makes a good beer, a tasty one but not strong, though it once proved too strong when we used to store it in the children's bedroom. James and Robert took a deal too much one evening, and spilt as big a quantity as they drank. Then they were up and down to the back all night long and half the next day. I didn't take the belt to them until they were recovered, and then not too hard. There's plenty of fathers would have taken it to them there and then and who wouldn't have spared it. I didn't let them mess up the privy though - that's really just for me and Alice, though James is now allowed to use it so long as he keeps it clean. The younger ones use the dug up bit of ground beyond the yard.

It's a hard life keeping them fed, trying to keep them clean, bringing them up with some decent Christian ways. Maybe I'll see if the boys can show any skill at this trade, and try to encourage them in it. My three boys can read better than I know how to, even George, who's only just seven. We're luckier than most villages, in that there's a free school for them, though James won't be going there for a great deal longer. Even the girls can get some learning at their cottage school, though Alice can't always spare Mary, the nine-year-old. She's the only girl old enough to be of help in the house, and there are times when there's more work to do than one pair of hands can manage. But then, learning's not too important for girls. Alice can barely read and yet she's a very capable wife.

The only worry I have is this - when I look at the stuff I make, these small things we live off, I often think - what happens if the fashions change? There's a good few of us around here making these things, a lot of families relying on the trade, and there's not much else for us if rich people decide they don't want to buy it anymore. I don't think that will happen, but then you can never tell. People are fickle, especially women.

The candle's in its last flickering moments now. I'll pinch the damn thing out and go inside. It'll be warm in that room and I'll eat with Alice and then get her to rest. There are always clothes to be made, clothes to mend, her days are even longer than mine. And I wouldn't swap with her either, this shed is a haven, rough though it is. The children know never to disturb me here, they know better than to make so much as a sound outside this door. Alice has got the little ones under her feet all day, and she frets about putting enough food on the table to feed bellies, about finding enough cloth to make decent garments to put them in. Still, women were intended to have children and to care for them, it's nature's way. Just as it's my task to provide the means.

Have a stroll sometime around our village. It's a prettier, cleaner place now. There are a few more houses of course, though far fewer people. That tells you something! The hills around are fine and glorious, though I never walked them much myself. Never had the time. They've covered most of the shafts now, so if you venture far out there, you should be in no danger. But of course the ways are steep and rough.

Take care, and God bless.

Magpie Mine

R.P. 2006

Historical Note

The once famous 'Ashford Black Marble' was not, in fact, a true marble, but a form of limestone. When it was polished up, this could be transformed from its natural grey to a deep glossy black.

Black Marble was ideal for being carved into ornaments, jewellery, decorations and even items of furniture. It proved very successful at the Great Exhibition of 1851, held at London's new Crystal Palace, and demand soared for all its products around that time. Most popular of all was the beautiful 'inlay' work of flowers or geometrical designs, which required great skill and care.

Ashford in the Water was the centre of this industry, the stone being mined locally and cut in an Ashford mill. Much of the trade was carried out by home-workers in the village, though larger workshops also existed. The teller of this tale is one such skilled craftsman, his family life and worries typical of many.

Black Marble remained very popular throughout Queen Victoria's reign. (The Queen's liking for black, during her widowhood, probably provided a very useful advert). But fashion was bound to change at some point, especially when cheaper jewellery became far more easily available. Both the quarry and the mill closed in 1905, though items continued to be made for a time, until the stock of marble ran out. The fame of the little village was past!

The Needle Girl's Tale

If I'm going to end up like my mother (and I probably am, why fool myself?) then I'm going to make sure I enjoy a bit of my life first.

Let me tell you about my mother. She must be thirty-six, which is old enough, but she looks a deal older. She's got six children still living and a face that no man's going to take a second glance at. Hard to imagine anyone ever did, but she tells me she had the pick of Hathersage at eighteen, not that it probably amounted to much, not if it's anything like now. She picked my pa, and it turned out to be a very bad choice because he was drunk for much of the time and shouting at us the rest. That's how I remember it, anyway. He died two years ago - grinders' disease, people said. I doubt you've ever heard of such a thing, so I'll tell you more of it in a moment.

I never mourned him and I'm sure she didn't either, even though we needed some help from that Poor Law Relief to get by. She did a bit of needle packing at home, but that didn't bring much in. Work done at home is even worse paid than here, and in any case she couldn't do a great deal with children around and a lot of other work to do. I was the oldest and I'd already been at work here a while. I was more than glad to be out of that schoolroom up the street. I'd had enough of reading, writing and adding up and the schoolmistress had probably had enough of me. I wasn't her favourite pupil. Now, most of what I earn goes to help feed the family. They need every penny I make, but they don't get it. I make sure I put a few coins each week into a box, and I keep that box well hidden. You've got to look after yourself.

Started here just before my thirteenth birthday - summer of 1842 - and since then I've been packing things - needles, hackle pins, gill pins - whatever it is that's sent into this back room from the factory through there. You wouldn't believe how many needles people must buy.

Some are even sent to foreign places, like France. Me and Doris have to put them all into little packets and then we wrap the best ones in fancy paper. Of course hackles and gill pins are used in the making of wool, and that's a very big industry nowadays.

There's hardly any women working in this place, and I'm the only girl here. It's nearly all boys and men - and no worse for that! Nice to get the eye when you walk through the workshops, and there's a good few of them that find some reason to come in here. They'll bring a box of pins, or something that got left behind, so they tell me. I know it's nonsense. One or two older men aren't above that sort of thing either. I don't bother to smile or say thank you unless it's someone I have a fancy for, and there's not so many of those. But I know it's me they want to see. Doris is well past being looked at - she's nearly thirty - and other than us there's only daft Joseph around the back here. He's not up to doing a proper man's job, like wire pulling or needle grinding. Course he's not paid much for just stacking boxes or loading them up onto carts out in the yard - mostly boxes filled with the little packets of needles that me and Doris have made up and then wrapped. We can do it almost without looking, and very fast too, if there's any one around that matters. Mr Cook is about at times - he's the owner of this manufactory - and then you wouldn't believe how fast our fingers move. Other times we slow down a bit and have a gossip, but we're never too slow because they count boxes going out of here at the end of each day. Mr Cook wouldn't be able to have his big house and his servants if he stood for any idleness, now would he? Barnfield House, it's called. We walked past it once, me and John, and I thought - no wonder we all have to work so hard. Six o'clock till six o'clock I'm in this room, and later if there's anything to be got out quickly. My fingers ache all night, once I stop. And they're covered in little cuts and scabs. We get a bit of a rest in the middle of the day, and I go out to the yard with my hunk of bread and bit of ham or bacon, and see if there's any one there worth chatting to.

No, I wouldn't say I enjoy it here, it's too hard and the day's too long, but at least I'm no one's servant and there's little work around for girls other than that. My friend Lizzie works as a maid over at North Lees Hall - that's another rich house not far from here. Lizzie's sixteen, like me, and she lives in. She has to make an even earlier start to the day than I do. A family called Eyre lives in that place, been there for a very long time, and at the moment there's a Mrs Eyre, with four of her children. None of them married and three of them over forty - can you imagine? Even the youngest is thirty-nine! Lizzie says Mrs Eyre is nice enough, but of course she doesn't see much of her, it's some miserable housekeeper that has her eye on Lizzie all day long and never stops finding fault. She has to be polite all the time, and do everything just so. I wouldn't be able to abide that. I like to speak my mind plainly, and you can say just what you think to people in this place. It wouldn't suit any one too fussy because you hear foul language often enough - though not when Mr Cook's around, he doesn't stand for it.

Of course Lizzie sometimes sees the sort of people I never come across. A woman was there a few weeks back, quite a well known person, Lizzie said, a writer - not that I'd ever heard of her. Brontë, she was called - odd name, that's why it's stuck in my mind. Arrived there with her friend from the vicarage - Ellen somebody - and they were borrowing a horse from Mrs Eyre. Lizzie was out in the yard emptying something when they were getting it saddled up. "Do take your time, Charlotte," pipes Mrs Eyre, "and have a lovely day, my dear." Must be very nice to have the time to take. Those sort of people don't know that places like this exist. It's not their world, is it? Lizzie says that Ellen has often been to the Hall, and not long ago she overheard her chatting to Mrs Eyre, while she was laying out some of tea for them. Ellen's brother is the vicar in Hathersage, and Ellen was saying he'd once proposed to this Charlotte Brontë! She turned him down, and now he's gone off and married someone else - someone quite rich. Anyway, Lizzie didn't think Charlotte looked the marrying sort, any more than that Ellen does. Very prim and proper, both of them, and none too young either.

There's plenty of men here in this factory of Mr Cook's. Some of them came in from other places with their families and the village has grown a bit since my mother was young. This isn't the only manufactory here - there's others in the village, all making much the same sort of thing as we do - wires, pins, needles, even umbrella frames. At one time, a long way back, this village was famous for making brass buttons - that was in Dale Mill. But nobody seems to want brass buttons now, so Dale Mill makes needles and pins, like the rest of us. The Atlas Works is just down the road and that's where John is, the one I might marry in a year or two, if nothing better comes my way. He's a grinder, like Pa was - there's a fair number of grinders in this place as well, but it's better that he's not been taken on here, right under my feet. Gives me a chance to keep my eyes open, and is there any reason why I shouldn't? After all, we're not married yet and life probably won't be much fun when we are. Once babies start to come, it's nothing but work and worries, isn't it? But I don't want to end up an old maid either, like Doris, that's much worse.

To be honest, John's not badly paid for the job he does, he's as well paid as anyone's going to be in this sort of place. The grinders would be a great deal better off if they didn't drink most of their wages! Course it's a very skilled job, grinding, not many can master it. A lot of boys try to learn when they reach fifteen or sixteen, but most of them never do it well enough. You've to hold fifty or more needle wires between your two hands, all placed out flat and straight. Then you need to roll them, not letting any drop, and at the same time push all the ends against the grindstone, which is what gets them sharp. If your fingers catch the stone it can rip the skin off them. Of course the grindstone's turning very very fast, so dust and grit and tiny bits of steel are all flying off right up into your face. All that stuff gets in your mouth and down your throat, but the windows are kept tight shut and they're covered with sticky dust, so it's quite dark in there as well. That's why my pa used to drink so much. He said he had to, or else his throat was dry and sore all the time and he could neither eat nor sleep. As I said, they all drink a lot, the grinders - when they're not working they're in The George or some other alehouse. John takes less than most of them, but then he's still trying to make sure of me. When he has, I don't doubt he'll be just like the rest.

Not long back they gave John some sort of mouth cover with a face screen fixed on it, but he doesn't use it - hardly any of them do. He says he'd rather tie a handkerchief round, and in any case the grinders all say they get paid well on account of it being such a bad job to do. If it wasn't so bad, there wouldn't be the same money in it.

Mind you, we all have to breathe in a lot of that dust and grit. The whole village is covered in the damn stuff and you can smell the black smoke coming out of this place from a good distance off. But the grinding room's the worst of all. I've only been in a couple of times but I could scarcely breathe.

John's a good grinder. He can sharpen up thousands of needle wires in an hour. He's even hoping to get Mr Cocker - that's the owner of Atlas Works - to pay him a shilling a week more. That would give us a decent wage to live on, even with children. What worries me, though, is that John's always coughing up and he's sick more often than most. It's a nasty colour, the phlegm he coughs up, dark brown and thick looking. He says it's nothing that a drink and a bit of fresh air won't cure, but sometimes of a summer evening, when we get out for a walk on the hills, he tires quite soon. Well I know that's often an excuse to make sure the two of us get lying down in some quiet spot together - he's not so ill that he doesn't want to do things like that. If it was down to him, there'd no doubt be one on its way already, and then we'd have to be married quicker than I'd choose. But it seems to me he doesn't have a strong look about him, not like some of the other ones I take notice of. And there's no grinder I know of that's more than forty and very few as old as that. Still, I suppose forty's not so young. It's a very long way off - John's barely twenty.

Must get on now. Work's been slow coming in today, but there's another lot of pins just arrived and I'm told they're to be ready and packed up by tonight, so they can be sent across by horse and cart to Bradford tomorrow. Must be going to some woollen mill.

Take a look around Hathersage sometime, if you can. It's fairly clean now and I don't doubt it smells a lot sweeter. Any dirt in the air these days is from cars, not from the making of goods. I doubt if anyone makes anything here any more. You could walk as far as North Lees Hall - of course the Eyres have all gone now and so have the servants. I'm told rich people stay there for holidays, so perhaps in some ways things haven't changed so much. That Brontë woman wrote a book and put North Lees Hall in it - Thornfield Hall, she called it. She used the name Eyre in the book as well.

If you should ever spend time wandering around these parts, just make sure you enjoy yourself! Life's short, and in my experience most of it's very hard.

Historical Note

During the 19th century, the small town of Hathersage was a real hive of industry. Once well known for the manufacture of brass buttons, by the middle of the century it was famous for its production of needles, pins and wire products. These were all manufactured in the town's several water-powered, and later steam-powered, mills.

Both adults and children were employed in the industry and often worked up to fifteen hours a day. One of the most unhealthy jobs must certainly have been 'needle grinding' (making sharp points on needles, by holding them against a revolving grindstone). This unpleasant task was done by the older boys and men, who worked at great speed and breathed in fine metal particles all day long. Not surprisingly, they usually developed lung disease very quickly. As the rather feisty girl who tells her tale here mentions, it was very rare for a grinder to live beyond the age of forty. Many did not survive the job for more than ten years.

Hathersage would certainly have presented a very different picture from the attractive place we see today - it would have been grimy, full of metal dust and covered at all times with a pall of black smoke from the mill chimneys.

NORTH LEES HALL

R.P 2006.

The Turnpike's Tale

Why such a fuss to be made over a few fleas? This house is no worse than most. Martha's very lucky if she's found decent, clean lodgings, as she says she has. Though I'd be surprised if a bit more hard looking doesn't unearth a good few fleas, and no shortage of bedbugs beside. Show me the clothing or blankets without them! Perhaps the bed coverings of the rich can be ridded of such pests, shaken out daily by servants and even washed now and then. But there's precious little most of us can do about a few red pimples or itching skin. And where's the worry?

Martha's always been haughty in her ways, and wilful. All too ready to turn up her nose at what I provide here. But it won't last long, not now she's working in Dale Mill. And if the woman she's found lodgings with has any sense, she won't put up with it either, no more than I've been prepared to. There's seven children in that house, and the father died two or three months back, taken suddenly with a burning throat and fever, as I understand. So Mrs Cartwright has more than enough on her plate, she'll be expecting Martha to be of help around the place, and not just by paying her keep either, no matter how many hours of work she's already had to do. There'll be no getting waited on in that house, and quite right. Perhaps it'll teach her a thing or two, because she's never seemed to want to take it from me, but it'll need well learning if she's to get herself married. There's not a man about who's going to put up with it. Perhaps if she'd had a mother worth the name, Martha would have grown up to be a different sort of girl.

A right royal row, we had, that night she told me she was leaving, made much worse by the day I'd endured. A day full of insults and abuse, even more than usual. And her not around to help, neither inside nor on the gate. Over in Hathersage she'd been, for all of the four days previous, finding herself a job and looking for lodgings, as I was later to hear, and beyond that no doubt mixing with God knows who and getting up to God knows what. Arrived back quite late in the evening - light was already starting to go - on some old farm wagon, a creaking one-horse thing. Had the boldness to ask me if the wagoner could pass through the gate without payment. I refused, not liking the look of the fellow one bit, but I may well

"Turnpike gate"

R.P 2006

have refused in any case. While I unlocked the gate, in no great rush, he shouted some lewd words towards her - words I am not prepared to repeat, though they were hardly new to me. Then, as he whipped his nag forward, he hurled the payment down to the ground. This is not an uncommon thing, of course. My back is a great problem to me, but it often has to be bent to pick up coins that have been flung carelessly - or spitefully - into the mud. If possible, I try to let the rider or wagon move well away before searching, so that no one watches my indignity, but not even the smallest coin can be ignored. There is no choice but to grovel and prod around in the wet earth, like a swine.

Martha's eyes fixed straight on mine that night, almost daring me to chastise her. "I've found myself work," she announces, "and a place to live. Sam will come by here tomorrow afternoon and take me back to Hathersage." Sam, I was left to guess, was the foul-mannered speciman that had just continued on his way. "I'll need nothing from you," she added hastily, no doubt judging that to be my first thought. "I'll be earning a wage, enough to pay for my bed and some food. Better than working in this filthy place and having nothing........." She stopped at that point, perhaps uneasy about the hardness in my look. Martha's had the stick taken to her often enough in the past, no doubt she feared me reaching for one now. I could not have been condemned for it. She was barely sixteen years, and had acted without my leave, without blessing. And if she went, I would be left here to work the gate alone, at the beck and call of travellers all day long, and at any time of the night they happened to choose. And without even the bit of money that came from her unwilling efforts on the spinning wheel. Her brother Will could hardly be of much help to me, as well she knew. The poor lad is good-natured enough, but not properly grown-up - a simpleton. It's all too easy for him to be tricked, and that's what's happened often enough, when I've left him to work the gate. It's an honest traveller who doesn't underpay him, or try to pay him not at all. And there are few honest travellers about, few indeed. Swindling the pikeman, as gatekeepers are often known, is a great sport for all. Even the rich and the important are not above it, in fact they are the guiltiest of all, so it seems to me.

Of course, there was nothing I could do to stop Martha going, short of locking her up or telling her she was never to appear at my door again. The first ploy could not have worked for very long, I am not a cruel man. Neither could the second, for she would merely have laughed and willingly agreed to such terms. I don't fool myself that she holds me in any great affection. In any case, I couldn't truly find the hardness in me to say it, angry as I was. There was something about her strong-minded ways that I grudgingly admired. But how much better for poor Will to have shown such spirit, not his twin sister! It can only make for difficulties in a girl.

Nonetheless, I could understand her dislike of this place - stranded out in wild country as we are, remote from everything a young woman might find of interest. Far from the gossip and chatter of neighbours, hidden from the admiring glances of young men. I don't include the travellers on the road in this thought. She receives many a crude invitation from that quarter, and not all of them would be refused, I'm fairly sure, if I was to risk leaving her here alone. "Get yourself to bed," I ordered, my eyes losing none of their glare. It is a mistake to reveal weakness to a woman, she will recognise it just like a bitch picking up on a scent. "We'll talk of this tomorrow." "There's no need for talk," came the bold reply. Although my hands were clenched, she must have known the moment of danger had passed.

The thought of Martha labouring for the owner of Dale Mill does not, in itself, trouble me. Work is the fate of all of us, excepting the rich. How they spend their days I have little idea. The only people of wealth I ever have business with are those who occasionally pay their toll at the gate, usually with bad grace, often with foul words. The ones who pass by in stage coaches have no need to utter a word, of course, and rarely do. Payment is made by the coachman, if at all. Sometimes he merely waves a ticket, paid for at some distant gate that belongs to the same Turnpike Trust. But both coachmen and passengers are quick to show their irritation, if they perceive any slowness in dealing with money or in opening the gate. I have taught myself to count, but not with speed, so it is rare to receive a cheery salute or a word of thanks.

But without doubt, for myself I would choose life here, against some more crowded place. I am not overly fond of people, and have reason not to be so. My mother died while giving birth to me - sixteen years old and not married to my father. A poor start, by anyone's reckoning. Something of a miracle I survived, and that thanks to a little generosity from the Parish of Sheffield. I was put into the care of a woman living in Ecclesall Bierlow, who had just lost a young child and was willing to become my wet nurse. She then kept me in her house, to grow up along with her own. It was certainly not kindness that inspired her, and why should it have been? The woman received a small weekly sum from the Parish, part of which was paid for by my dead mother's employer, the master of a house of reasonable substance in that place. Following my birth, he signed a bond with the Parish authorities, promising - should I survive - to pay an annual sum for ten years towards my keep, and this he honoured. I presume that man to have fathered me. We never once spoke and I have no idea now whether he is alive or dead. Nor do I care.

The bastard child is not looked upon warmly, though there are a very great number around, both then and now. My childhood was a hard one, not spent in affection and not remembered with it. Perhaps that's why I attempted to avoid a similar fate for my own. The day Bess told me she was carrying my child, I offered to marry her in some haste, a decision I quickly relented of. The girl was impoverished, already the mother of a boy lost to smallpox at a few months old, whose father had abandoned her. Life for such girls is cruel, and many of them prostitute themselves, at a young age. Bess was no doubt further along that course than I could have imagined. Although about thirty years old, I was little experienced in such matters.

Whether she was honest in claiming me responsible, I was soon far from sure. But it could have been so. By some miracle, she survived the long and difficult births of Martha and Will, but our son was born many hours after his sister, and he was not born right. The boy will never be a proper man, and I have stopped praying to God that he will be. There is no help for it.

I was given no schooling and had always laboured on the land, wherever work could be found. But by the time of my marriage, such labour was ever harder to come by. The food in our bellies depended on the goodwill of farmers, on the harvest, the weather, the seasons, on good fortune. And poor people like us could no longer even graze a cow, or a couple of scraggy sheep, on the open land. This had all been stolen - and walled in - by the already rich and greedy. Our Common Land was gone - we were at the mercy of land-owners and whatever bits of work they chose to offer.

There was no certainty in such a livelihood and more times than not my family was hungry and ill-clad. Bess must have found herself tempted back towards the easier earnings of the prostitute, that low form of life never far from anyone's door. No doubt I was to blame. When Martha and Will were around two years old, the winter was harsh. For weeks on end, I had no work, none at all. Once again the Parish had to come to my aid, a shame which caused me to burn with helpless anger. Bess got no hand of support from me, only bitter words. I was too ill-fed and far too wretched even to share my body with her for comfort.

There's no good cure for that disease. No doubt I was lucky to have lost all desire for her. Some man, from whom she earned an easy coin or two, must have passed the cursed thing to her, and then she, as surely, to others. A neighbour obtained mercury for Bess and the poor creature dosed herself, again and yet again. It did not take long for her teeth to loosen and then to be lost, barely longer for her fair hair to fall out in handfuls. The mercury was surely to blame, but what else can be done? At times it seems to bring a cure. But a truly monstrous and pitiable sight, my Bess soon was, scorned by any who set eyes on her. Jeered at, even by pauper children in the street. But the poisonous draughts did not bring her a cure - Bess died just after Martha and Will reached their third birthday. I have to say, in shame, that she was not mourned.

I have never wished to marry again, and almost certainly never will. The chance to come here, about six years ago, to this lonely place, away from the gossips and the scandal mongers, was very welcome. Autumn of 1795, it was. By hard work and a slight change in my luck, I had managed by then to scrape together a modest sum - enough to put in a bid at the auction for this toll box - a simple home, just two small rooms built hard against the roadside. One room has a window jutting out into the road itself, intended to ease the handing over of money, but I don't use it often. In all but the very worst weather I choose to sit outside, under a simple porch I built myself, looking at the world about me and listening for the sound of hooves or a rumble of wheels. This is greatly more pleasant than being indoors, in that small, dingy room, smelling of damp, even when the fire's lit. Will sits with me quite often, chattering idly and to no purpose, sometimes announcing the approach of travellers when there are none. On occasions, he does simple farm labouring, but only when workers are in short supply, which is rare. He'll be here with me until the day I die, but after that, God knows. I shall try to leave Martha a little money for his benefit, and hope that she may care for him. If she chooses not to be honourable, then I dread to think what will become of Will. He will be dependent on the Parish, and if the Parish so decides, he could spend the rest of his days in an asylum.

I hope Martha will lead a decent life in that village, and not give herself to any loutish lad or bullying man that crosses her path. A girl living away from home, even in decent lodgings, will be seen as easy prey, and Mrs Cartwright will hardly have the time, or even the inclination, to keep a check. I've heard the owner of Dale Mill is firm and strict, so I trust he will allow no lewd behaviour in that place. No doubt he is concerned that the workers produce him his brass buttons, without any wasting of their time, and thus keep him in wealth. But Martha is a child no longer, she must take the consequences of her actions. There's no way I can help her now, if she should choose a wayward path.

Perhaps she's right. Perhaps it will give her a better life. This place is damp and bug-ridden, Martha's right about that, though I cannot imagine her new arrangements being much different. Not that I'll have occasion to view them, not at any time I can foresee. The gate can't be abandoned, only if you're prepared to lose money by leaving it open and I'm not, no more than I'll risk leaving Will here on his own. There's toll boxes been broken into that I've heard about, there's even been gatekeepers murdered before now. People must imagine there's a deal of money hoarded inside these places, but there's never very much here, not once I've paid out for the lease. And of course this is a hard road, a steep and very lonely one, hazardous in places. Even now, there's many who won't attempt it outside summer, so my profits are not steady. That's why the gate went cheaply at auction. I've thought about keeping a large dog here to protect us, as many toll keepers do, but a dog has a mouth to feed like anyone else. You can't rely on it always catching rabbits.

Much as the tolls are resented, there's no doubt at all that turnpikes have made the roads better. Forty years ago, so I'm told, for much of the year there was barely a passable road this side of Sheffield. And most roads then hardly merited the name - they were nothing but rough tracks, rutted and dusty in summer, marshy and treacherous in winter. Very few would have ventured this far out at that time, not until they turnpiked the road from Sheffield out to Castleton, and on towards Manchester. Year of 1758, that was started. But even now, travelling can be a dangerous thing, and it's costly - not something most people manage very often, if at all. I've only done that journey the once myself, eight years back, and I've no particular wish to endure it again. Six in the morning, I set off from Sheffield, grim enough day, it was, with a chilling wind. I was seated on the outside of the coach - it's cheaper there - armed with nothing more than a few hunks of bread and a small flask of spirit. Not far beyond Sheffield, we were, and that curse of a coachman nearly lost control of the thing, going down

Callow Bank - horses sliding about everywhere in the mud. Through Hathersage, we went, and he had to change two lame horses there, then on to Mytham Bridge - that's near here. After that we were heading out for Hope and Castleton and then, of course, up that infernal hill called Winnats Pass. Able-bodied passengers are expected to get out and walk up there, but even so it's not unusual for a horse to collapse dead. A coach horse only has a working life of three or four years out here, and that's no surprise.

Desolate place, Winnats is. The very year the road was turnpiked, a young lad and lass were murdered on that Pass, and their corpses thrown down into the Speedwell Mine. It's a true tale that lives on in people's fears. I doubt there's a traveller who isn't well relieved to be over the top of Winnats and heading down the other side, towards Chapel. Bitterly cold it was, too, up there. My body was in pain with it for the rest of the journey. Around ten o'clock at night, when we finally reached Manchester. But at least it could be done, and done in a day. Not like before.

Yes, turnpikes have been a boon for travellers - there's even a stagecoach now from Sheffield that can get you to London in twenty-six hours! Very hard to believe, but I'm told it's true. The tolls take money to maintain the roads, even improve them. Before that, of course, it was every able-bodied man in each parish, forced to do his bit for a few days a year. But not every parish made a decent job of it, and outside the towns you didn't find anything better than packhorse tracks. Decent highways cost money, and at the gate we have a board, showing who has to pay what, because there's a different rate for riders, carts, stagecoaches and so on. A man on foot gets through free, but there are very few on this road out here. The Mail Coach never has to pay either - its coachman will blow his horn from a good distance and the gate has to be thrown open quickly, or there's a lot of angry shouting. Wagons with narrow wheels have to pay more, because they do more damage to the road. That can cause a lot of bad feeling, when people have to wait while you measure up. I'm not obliged to give anyone change, but I keep a few coins in an old leather bag, strapped round my waist. Occasionally, a traveller will refuse it, cursing it as not fit to handle. One such came by not more than a few days back - in a private chaise. It's very rare you see a chaise out this way, but it was a bright, warm day and the arrogant fellow was no doubt showing off his prowess to the young woman sitting at his side. "Pikeman!" he shouts towards me, as I started to rise slowly from my stool - for even that I can't do without pain. "Throw this gate open, and do it fast!"

He was driving the horse - an over-excited thing, probably a stallion - hard against the gate and its front hooves were kicking into the wood. A gloved hand dropped money into my palm, while the woman stared away from me. I was too lowly a thing to rest her gaze upon. "Don't soil me with your filthy coins!" says he, as my hand went into the bag for a small piece of change, and I heard her laugh as the stallion was given its head. "May that creature hurl you both to the ground," I thought sourly. "And may the landing be painful."

Martha's been gone some three months now. At times I miss the sight of her about the place, but not her discontent, or her loud, complaining tones. It's doubtless best she's no longer here - this place offers little to a woman, even less to a girl. Will and I are content enough together. We don't feel hunger often - bread comes out to us with the carts, vegetables too sometimes, and Will can even manage to cook a tasty enough broth. I'm at ease with the sound of his idle chatter, which demands no response, and with his excitement at the approach of horses. I find a comfort in the noisy way he gulps his soup, and even in his steady snoring throughout the hours of darkness. Perhaps he is a gift to me, after all.

So I shall carry on taking payments for this lonely roadway, until I'm too old not to be ignored or robbed. There's even a little money getting put aside, and buried safely in the ground behind the house. Enough, I trust, to save us both from the loveless mercies of the Parish.

Historical Note

Until the late 18th century, roads throughout England were in very poor condition and usually impassable in bad weather. Journeys were therefore slow and often dangerous. It was becoming clear that something would have to be done.

Turnpiking was seen as a good way to raise money, both to improve roads and to extend them. Turnpike roads were run by Trusts, which usually consisted of landowners and other influential people. Each Trust had to be authorised by Parliament, and it could then set up toll gates, or pikes, along agreed routes. The Trust would build a small house by each gate for the toll collector, and often the lease for a gate was sold at auction.

In his 'Pickwick Papers', Charles Dickens describes toll keepers as 'men that 'as met with some disappointment in life, consequence of which they retires from the work and shuts themselves up in pikes; partly with the view of being solitary and partly to revenge themselves on mankind by taking tolls'. Toll keepers were renowned for being surly, but they were generally resented and often abused, as the teller of this tale complains!

The Peak District was criss-crossed with turnpike roads and a good number of old toll houses survive. Some have been converted into attractive country cottages, which can often be recognised by the closeness of a wall or bay window to the road. The turnpike system lasted until 1888, when local government took over responsibility for roads.